Racing with the Hawk

The Man behind Dale Earnhardt

Jerome Lucido

Fleming H. Revell
A Division of Baker Book House
Grand Rapids, Michigan 49516

Published by Fleming H. Revell
a division of Baker Book House Company
P.O. Box 6287, Grand Rapids, MI 49516-6287

Third printing, September 1998

Printed in the United States of America

Library of Congress Cataloging-in-Publication Data

Lucido, Jerome, 1943–
    Racing with the hawk : the man behind Dale Earnhardt / Jerome
Lucido.
      p. cm.
    Includes bibliographical references (p.).
    ISBN 0-8007-5657-6
    1. Hawk, Don. 2. Earnhardt, Dale, 1951– . 3. Automobile racing
drivers—United States—Biography. 4. Stock car racing—United States.
I. Title.
GV1032.E18L83 1998
796.72'092—dc21   97-48349

For current information about all releases from Baker Book House, visit our web site:
http://www.bakerbooks.com

For Bonnie,
who blessed me
with her goodness, sweetness, and love

Contents

Foreword

In NASCAR racing circles, the name Don Hawk is almost as well-known as Dale Earnhardt. Hawk is the president of Dale Earnhardt Inc., the man who, along with Dale and Teresa Earnhardt, directs the business activities of the Man in Black. The Intimidator. Winner of the 1998 Daytona 500 (a title that eluded him nineteen seasons) and the only driver besides Richard Petty to win seven Winston Cup Championships.

Hawk, a no-nonsense negotiator known for his honest business dealings, negotiates Earnhardt's sponsorship and endorsement contracts and licensing deals—a financial empire that approaches Michael Jordan proportions. With Hawk handling much of his business, Earnhardt has made more money than even he could have dreamed.

But Hawk brings more to NASCAR than his business savvy. He brings his solid Christian lifestyle to the racing scene, affecting hundreds of people on and off the track. He shows what an honest, capable, Christian man can accomplish in a hard-driving world.

Racing with the Hawk takes a behind-the-scenes look at a typical Winston Cup season through the eyes of Don Hawk and tells the story of one of NASCAR's most highly regarded figures. The key to success is surprisingly the same for both the hard-charging Earnhardt in his black Monte Carlo, and Hawk, his Bible-college-educated president of operations.

—The Publisher

Don Hawk: Kingdom Builder

Daytona Beach, Florida

It's a warm, summerlike afternoon in Florida—even though it is the middle of February. The sky is deep blue. A few wispy clouds pass high overhead. The fragrance of jasmine floats on a gentle breeze.

It's a perfect day for a race.

The stands at Daytona International Speedway are filled to capacity with nearly two hundred thousand people, hundreds of whom are waving banners and wearing patches bearing the number three in honor of their hero: The Intimidator, Dale Earnhardt. Everywhere, it seems, there are seas of black flags emblazoned with the number of his black Monte Carlo. Earnhardt, a seven-time Winston Cup champion, is the clear favorite of this crowd.

A few years earlier, the crowd would have belonged to Richard Petty, and his number forty-three would have been flapping in the breeze. But Petty has retired to politics and

Earnhardt has ascended to the throne as undisputed king of NASCAR racing. He holds the position to some degree because of the shrewd negotiating and management practices of a man named Don Hawk, the president of Dale Earnhardt Inc.

On this midwinter afternoon, Earnhardt is trying, for the eighteenth time, to capture the one NASCAR jewel that has managed somehow to elude his grasp—the Daytona 500. Earnhardt has won twenty-eight other NASCAR races here, but never this annual opening event of the Winston Cup season. And this may be the year.

Coming into this race weekend, everything seemed to be going Earnhardt's way. A week earlier, he had breezed to victory in the International Race of Champions here in what seemed to be a tuneup for his first checkered flag in the 500.

The roar of the huge crowd is dwarfed by the explosion of noise from the engines catapulting around the 2.5-mile multioval track at speeds approaching 200 miles per hour. For much of the race, Earnhardt seems well on his way to victory—but he cannot seem to pull away from Dale Jarrett, who matches him turn for turn, lap for lap.

Tension is building as the race heads into its final 25 laps. Jarrett's Ford Thunderbird is still on Earnhardt's tail, so close it would be hard to wedge a piece of paper between them. Only fractions of a second behind are Ken Schrader, Mark Martin, Jeff Burton, Wally Dallenbach Jr., and Ted Musgrave in a close pack.

Earnhardt is a master at protecting a lead, and he seems to have a sixth sense regarding every effort Jarrett makes to overtake him. Jarrett's Thunderbird, with its powerful Robert Yates–built engine, has the horsepower to overtake the black Monte Carlo, but wherever Jarrett tries to go, Earnhardt blocks him.

Jarrett moves inside. But Earnhardt is already there.

He tries a cut to the outside. Somehow, Earnhardt gets there first.

Twenty-four laps to go.

Meanwhile, Down in the Pit

In the pit, watching it all unfold, Don Hawk stands quietly focused on the track. He seems excited, but Don Hawk always seems to be excited. Even when he stands still, which isn't often, his body exudes nervous energy. And today, he's not standing still. He paces. He jabs the air with his fist when he sees Earnhardt make a blocking move. He seems to be every bit as much into the race as the man piloting the black Monte Carlo.

The noise is deafening and the activity frenzied as members of Earnhardt's crew get ready for the next pit stop. They know that a few seconds too many in the pit can be the difference between finishing first or second for even the best driver. And that difference can be measured in hundreds of thousands of dollars.

Hawk seems comfortable in the midst of the noise, confusion, and fumes. Obviously, he's very much at home here. He has one of the best-known names on the NASCAR circuit, yet it rarely appears in the newspaper or is heard on ESPN. He gets no glory or headlines, but everyone close to NASCAR knows he is a force in Dale Earnhardt Inc. The business machine he and Dale and Teresa Earnhardt run together is as smooth, powerful, and efficient as any race car Earnhardt has guided around a NASCAR track.

Hawk is pulling for his boss to win the Daytona 500, not only because it is one of the most prestigious events in racing but also because it will be wonderful for Earnhardt to get this monkey off his back.

Still, Hawk knows that Earnhardt's kingdom will not rise or fall based on a first-, second-, or even last-place finish in any one race. Besides, Hawk has his priorities in order: God first, family second, and then racing. He has a strong, unshakable faith in God which gives him a deep inner peace. That faith has carried him through some desperately trying times. It has kept him going as he has encountered the tragedy and loss that, sooner or later, touches all who make their living on the NASCAR circuit.

13

Pedal to the Metal

On the track, Jarrett has managed to move alongside Earnhardt. The two drivers are giving it everything they've got with pedal to the metal at more than 190 miles per hour.

The crowd is standing, roaring its approval. Even with more than 23 laps remaining, it seems certain that what happens in the next few seconds will determine the outcome of the race.

Earnhardt . . . Jarrett.

Now Jarrett . . . and Earnhardt.

And moving up quickly is Dallenbach.

Dallenbach is right on Jarrett's back bumper. He taps him and that seems to be just what Jarrett needs. The bump propels him forward—an extra burst that pushes him past Earnhardt and into the lead. Dallenbach falls back and is quickly swallowed by heavy traffic, dropping to fourth, fifth, and now sixth place.

But Earnhardt isn't called The Intimidator for nothing. He knows how to keep a lead, and he knows how to get one back. And today, everyone expects he will try anything to get even with Jarrett for what he did to Earnhardt here three years ago. In that race, Earnhardt led almost the entire distance before Jarrett passed him in the first turn of the last lap.

But no matter what Earnhardt tries today, nothing seems to work. Though he bumps, gouges, and pushes, Jarrett maintains the lead. Earnhardt stays with Jarrett the entire distance, but the Ford crosses the finish line just .12 seconds ahead of Earnhardt's Chevy—earning Jarrett $362,000 for the win.

For Earnhardt, the outcome is familiar. It's his fourth second-place finish in the Daytona 500.

A jubilant but exhausted Jarrett tells reporters, "That last lap was close to 500 miles in itself. I would rather look in my mirrors and see anyone but the 3-car behind me."

The last 15 laps of the race "were the most racking I've ever run, knowing Dale was behind me, knowing he was planning every trick he could think of to get by."

Earnhardt is disappointed but philosophical. "We just didn't have enough for him today. It was a good race."

14

No Time for Standing Still

Down in the pit with Earnhardt's crew, Don Hawk tensed as the cars approached the finish line, and exhaled sharply as he saw Jarrett take the checkered flag. He gave a slight, almost imperceptible shake of his head and quickly turned to other matters.

For Hawk, there is always some new business to attend to. As president and general manager of Earnhardt's multimillion-dollar business empire, his life consists of fourteen-hour days, many of them spent on the road away from his family.

Still, he doesn't seem to mind all that much. Nor do his wife, Cyndee, or children, Jessie, Julie, Jenny, and John. They understand—or try to—that racing has been an important part of his life since high school days. They know there is nothing else he would rather do, with the possible exception of being a preacher.

Hawk had planned, in fact, to be a preacher, but it took only a few days visiting a seminary to discover that wasn't the road he really wanted to take. And so the church's loss has been Dale Earnhardt's gain.

Late Sunday night after the Daytona 500, Earnhardt, Hawk, and the rest of their entourage boarded their Lear jet for the short flight back to North Carolina and Earnhardt's headquarters on a four-hundred-acre farm near Mooresville, a short drive from Charlotte.

Hawk knew he would need to be in the office early Monday morning to begin dealing with the dozens of faxes and priority mail packages from all over the country that regularly litter his desk. It seems that just about everyone in the country wants a piece of Dale Earnhardt. To get it, one must go through Don Hawk.

Sitting on his desk after Daytona were more than three hundred requests for personal appearances, and those were only the ones that arrived in the previous couple of weeks. Filed away are thousands of requests of various kinds, including one from a widow who wanted Earnhardt to drive the hearse for

15

her husband's funeral. More thousands of letters ask for autographed trading cards.

With Hawk at the helm, Dale Earnhardt Inc. has grown from its inception in 1979 to the point where it racks up an estimated fifty million dollars in souvenir sales each season. More than ten thousand General Motors dealerships sell Earnhardt-endorsed items, and Earnhardt's own catalog lists nearly eight hundred items for sale.

But it's not money that drives Hawk and Earnhardt. It's racing and the determination not only to be the best but to stay the best.

In a sport as competitive and changeable as NASCAR racing, getting to the top is not easy. It's even harder to stay there.

Garrow on Hawk

Mark Garrow, television and radio analyst: Don Hawk is someone who will deal honestly with you and give you answers, even in the toughest situations. He's a man who really wants to do the best he can for the people he represents.

He's certainly one of the power brokers in racing right now because he represents Dale Earnhardt, but you never see him acting like a big shot. There have been times when I've called him about something and he's said, "I don't have time to talk to you right now, but you can call me at home tonight if you want to."

He doesn't mind letting people intrude on his personal time, and you don't find too many people who are like that. There are very few people who are so willing to give of themselves to others.

Don Hawk and Dale Earnhardt don't seem very much alike, but if people knew Dale, they would know that he and Don are very close in their thinking—especially regarding their faith and their outlook on life.

About the only people I can think of who might have something negative to say about Don are those who've tried to take a shortcut and failed to represent their client in the best way, or who have dealt in a way that was detrimental to the people Don represents. That's because Don stands up for the people he represents and for what he believes to be right.

In a day when people are willing to do what is expedient even if it is wrong, or sacrifice what they really believe in, Don is a refreshing change. He is determined to do the right thing. And that's rare.

Racing in the Blood

Rockingham, North Carolina

Exactly one week after losing to Dale Jarrett in the final laps of the Daytona 500, Dale Earnhardt is turning the tables on him.

Today, in the Goodwrench Service 400 at the North Carolina Motor Speedway, Jarrett took the lead early and held it most of the way. Until now. Just as he appears certain to start the Winston Cup season with two straight victories, Earnhardt's black Monte Carlo zips around him late in the race. Earnhardt breezes the rest of the way home to win the sixty-ninth checkered flag of his NASCAR career.

This time it is Jarrett's Thunderbird crossing the line in second place.

In victory lane, Don Hawk is jubilant. He's never one to boast or gloat, but the expression on his face shows that this victory feels good—especially after the disappointment of the previous week.

It's the kind of day that reminds him why he was attracted to racing all those years ago as a twelve-year-old living in his hometown of Allentown, Pennsylvania. A Saturday night activity for the Hawk family in the '60s was watching stock cars run around the small blacktop oval at Dorney Park. Fishbowl racing would be a better way to describe it because the track was so small. But every week without fail, Don, his mother, father, and two sisters were there.

It's a Long Way from Dorney Park

A smile comes to Don's face when he remembers what it was like back then and how far he's come.

"When I think about those two-hundred-dollar cars skidding around a small racing oval in Allentown and compare it to standing in the pit area at Daytona watching Dale's 700-horsepower Monte Carlo roar down the backstretch, I have to pinch myself and ask, 'Is this really happening? Is it really happening to me?'"

The transition from racing small-town stockers to competing at Daytona International Speedway is not made easily or quickly by anyone, and for young Don Hawk it wasn't even a dream. As a kid, he didn't spend much time fantasizing about slipping through the driver's window of a Ford or Chevy road rocket, strapping himself between the massive steel roll bars and thundering across the banked ovals of Talladega, Dover, and Pocono raceways. He just liked racing. Liked, in fact, everything about it. He liked the cars, the tracks, the drivers, the speed, the excitement as the cars tried to negotiate the tight turns at Dorney Park. He wanted to be as close to the action as possible.

While the rest of his family was content to view the race from the grandstand, nothing would do for Don but being down on the infield with the drivers and their crews. He was able to get what he wanted because his sister's boyfriend would sneak Don into the track area as the boy huddled on the floor of his tow truck.

The problem was that Don kept up a running monologue, even while his sister's boyfriend was trying to sneak him in.

"Man, this is fun, but it makes me nervous. How close are we to the gate? Is it coming up? What if they catch us; they won't catch us, will they? But what should I say if—"

"Don! Would you please lie still and be quiet!"

"Yeah, okay, okay. I'm trying to be still, but I just hope we don't get caught, you know. I don't want—"

"Will you please shut up! We're almost to the gate."

It wasn't easy for Don to quit talking or be still. As anyone who knows him can attest, it still isn't. Somehow, because he wanted it so desperately, Don managed to be quiet long enough to get past the security guard. But that was only half the battle. He still had to lie low and keep out of sight until dark. Only when the track lights came on could he get out and walk around. Usually, that wasn't until fifteen or twenty minutes after their arrival at the track, which seemed like an eternity to a young boy bubbling with excitement and energy.

But as soon as the first race started, it was worth every moment of discomfort and anxiety on the floor of that tow truck.

He Loved It All, Even the Dust

What Don experienced at track level was thrilling: the roar of the engines, the smell of gas fumes and burning oil, the pulse-pounding excitement as the cars tried to outmaneuver and out-muscle each other to reach the finish line first. He even loved the choking sensation from the tire rubber the cars threw up as they thundered past.

Don knew early on that he wanted to be part of the racing scene, and he was—first, as a spectator at Dorney Park, then working in the concession stands at Nazareth Raceway a few miles east of Allentown. By the time he was eighteen or nineteen years old, he had his own dirt-modified race car.

21

Then it was time for him to go to college to prepare for a career that had nothing to do with racing. Or so he thought.

Don had been sure of his calling since the summer of his sophomore year at Emmaus High School. He had grown up in a Christian family. But until that summer, he had never thought seriously about what it meant to be a Christian, or what it meant to truly surrender one's life to the lordship of Christ.

But at a Bible camp that year, he committed his life to Christ—lock, stock, and socket wrench. And as he did, he felt that he was also committing himself to a life spent in Christian service. It seemed a natural fit because Don liked people, loved to talk, and didn't shy away from being in the spotlight. It seemed certain that his future lay in serving God as a preacher in a local church.

Don was so sure of the direction his life was going to take that he refused a partial scholarship from the University of Delaware without giving it a second thought. He chose to attend Philadelphia College of Bible, a small interdenominational institution in center-city Philadelphia dedicated to preparing students for careers as preachers, missionaries, and Christian teachers.

Next Stop: The Ministry

Becoming a preacher of the gospel was something Don wanted, and, just as important, something his family wanted for him. They all believed the cars and racing would pass from the scene without regret. Racing was exciting, yes, but it could not begin to compare with the thrill of knowing he was doing exactly what God wanted him to do, that he was doing something of eternal importance.

But even as Don pursued a career in the ministry, he could not put cars and racing completely behind him.

Because he was always hanging around the Dankel Chevrolet dealership in downtown Allentown and it was obvious to all that he knew a great deal about cars, they eventually put him to work. By the time he was a senior in high school, he was their detail man, washing and buffing cars, a job he proudly carried out to perfection.

"In no time they bumped me up to prepping the new cars that came in," he remembers. "After that, they put me into dispatch because I knew a lot about the mechanics of a car and had a way with people."

While he was still in high school, he ended up running the entire shop after the service manager became seriously ill and had to be away from the job for several weeks. Don learned the computer system from the only other person at the dealership who understood it—computers then being new and mysterious to most people.

One morning Don reported to work and heard the shocking and upsetting news that his computer mentor had unexpectedly collapsed and died at home the night before. Though he didn't like the way it had happened—through the serious illness of one person and the death of another—at the age of eighteen, Don suddenly was vital to Dankel Chevrolet. He knew so many facets of the business that everyone expected him to step into a comfortable niche with the dealership. He could be secure and make a comfortable living. If he wanted to preach once in a while on Sunday morning, perhaps for a small church that couldn't afford a full-time preacher, that would be fine. But as far as his bosses and coworkers were concerned, he would be a fool to pass up the golden opportunity that had been dumped in his lap.

Don disagreed. And when he told his bosses he still planned to attend Bible college so he could become a preacher, they looked as if they thought he'd inhaled a few too many gas fumes at the racetrack.

"You're only eighteen years old! Do you know how many kids your age would do anything to be in your shoes?" they asked him.

He shrugged. "I haven't thought that much about it."

"Look, you love cars, and here's a chance to spend your life around them. Besides, do you realize how much money you'll be making? Right out of high school, you have the opportunity to make more in your first year than you'll ever make as a preacher."

Don wasn't tempted.

"That doesn't matter to me," he said. "I'm not going into the ministry because it's a way to make money. I'm doing it because I believe it's what God wants for me . . . and because I want to help people get closer to him."

His friends at Dankel tried another tactic. They nodded, smiled, shook his hand, and told him they knew he would be a success at whatever he did. If he had his heart set on being a preacher, they were sure he'd be a great one. And to show how much he was appreciated, they gave him a company car—a loaded Caprice Classic—to drive to school and back. The only catch was that they wanted him to work for them on weekends during the school year, when he was home for Christmas and spring break, and, of course, during the summer. They even promised to pay for his gas. They were betting he would eventually change his mind and return home to work for the dealership full time. Certainly, that beautiful Caprice would be a daily reminder of how nice a life that could be.

And so, for his entire four years in college, Don drove from Philadelphia to Allentown nearly every weekend to work at Dankel. On Sundays, he went to church in the morning, spent afternoons at work, and then headed back for the evening service. After that, it was another sixty miles down the Pennsylvania Turnpike to school for another week of classes.

Although Don enjoyed working at the dealership, his enthusiasm for the ministry never waned. And so, when graduation day finally came in 1977, he turned in the keys to his company car and hit the interstate, driving his parents' motor home in the direction of Dallas with four college buddies. They planned an inspection tour of Dallas Theological Seminary, having heard it was the place to go for a top-notch theological education. They wanted to see it for themselves before applying for admission. Some of their professors at Philadelphia Bible— men they respected and admired—had received their Master of Theology degrees from the seminary, and that added to Don's desire to enroll there.

He and his buddies were happy and excited about the experiences that awaited them, and during an early stop for gas, one of the young men bought cigars for all the guys as a means of celebrating their freedom from college life.

Don chuckles at the memory, because none of them was a smoker. "It was kind of like he was making a statement. He was saying, 'We light up these babies, guys, and break with some of the rules of the past four years.' But none of us smoked to begin with, and we certainly weren't going to start with twenty-five-cent cigars. We never even lit the things."

They reached Dallas in the middle of the night, so Don parked the motor home in the school parking lot, and he and his friends slept there. Early the next morning, they woke to the sound of someone rapping sharply on the door. Don opened it and found himself facing Dr. Charles Ryrie, chairman of the seminary's graduate school of theology, and author and editor of a number of books, including *The Ryrie Study Bible*. Ryrie had noticed the out-of-state license plate and wondered if he could offer any assistance. When he learned Don and his friends were there to check out the seminary, he bought their lunches and invited them to attend his church on Sunday.

Don could hardly believe that someone of such importance, a man so highly regarded in Christian circles, was so down-to-earth, friendly, and generous—especially to people he had never met. Certainly, this gentle man did more than speak and write about the Christian life. He lived it.

Dr. Ryrie's hospitality was a great beginning to a tour that confirmed everything Don and his friends already believed about Dallas Theological Seminary. This was definitely the place to study for the ministry. The faculty said it was so. The thousands of volumes in the school library echoed the thought. Everything about the place spoke of dedication and commitment to the gospel. It was just what Don and his friends were looking for.

Unexpected U-Turn

And yet, the more Don explored the campus, the more unsettled he felt inside. He sensed that his thinking about the ministry was changing. By the time his short stay in Dallas ended, he knew he wasn't going to apply for admission there or anywhere else.

One of his friends saw the disappointment in Don and tried to console him. "Hey . . . don't sweat it, man. This isn't the right place for everybody."

But Don knew his dismay had nothing to do with choosing the right seminary. He would never be attending seminary, and after four years of being certain this was his destiny, he suddenly felt lost and adrift. What was he going to do with his life now?

"Rock-solid sure as I had been for the previous six years that God had called me into church work . . . that's how convinced I became that seminary and an eventual pulpit weren't for me. At least not at that time."

Even twenty years later, he struggles for words to explain how he could make a 180-degree turn like that in such a short time. He still has trouble understanding exactly what happened. For a while after he decided not to enter the ministry, he questioned whether he was turning away from God's call. The last thing he wanted was to be disobedient.

"I was in that confusing position so many Christians find themselves in when they're questioning God's leading in life."

He wondered if he had mistaken as a call to the pastorate the powerful emotions that were part of his commitment to Christ while in high school.

"I wondered if I had nurtured those feelings for another six years, literally right up to the threshold of seminary training, only to discover that I had equally strong emotions about not becoming a preacher.

"The most important question for me was whether this was truly God's doing or mine."

Don told himself this major change of direction had to be the Lord's work—but he just wasn't sure. He was especially worried about how quickly his attitude had changed. How could he be so confident about going into the ministry one

26

moment and then—zap!—be just as convinced it wasn't the place for him? He wondered if he was like the double-minded man of whom James wrote in the New Testament, "That man should not think he will receive anything from the Lord" (James 1:7 NIV).

For Don, "The trip back from Dallas to Allentown gave me time for a serious reality check. The more I thought about it, the more I was sure I had done the right thing. I held onto that conviction in spite of the disappointment written all over my dad's face when I told him. He wanted me in the pulpit, not in the car business.

"It wasn't an easy time for me, yet looking back—and don't we all have great hindsight?—I realize the Lord wasn't saying, 'No,' to a ministry for me. It was more like, 'Not here, Don, and not now.'"

Twenty years later, Don can see that he was, indeed, traveling the path the Lord had set before him. But for a while after his return from Dallas, the way was neither clear nor easy to follow.

Wagenhals on Hawk

Fred Wagenhals, CEO, Action Performance Company: Don Hawk is a fair, aggressive, hardworking guy. I've always had a sense that he loves what he's doing, and if you like what you're doing, you get to be good at it. Don is very good at what he does. He loves the sport he's in, he likes working for the people he's working for, and he is a good, tough negotiator.

One thing that is really great about Don is that he's fair on both sides of the table. I think he realizes that when the deal is done, if it's not a good situation for both parties involved, it's not going to last very long and his reputation is going to be gone.

Dale Earnhardt is an aggressive racer, probably the best who's ever run that circuit, and Don is smart enough to have seen how to take Dale to the next level. I think he's mapped out a strategy to get Dale to that next marketing plateau.

I don't know anything in the business realm that I would change about Don, because he's probably the cream of the crop in terms of agents or business managers. That's not to belittle anybody else. It's just that Don Hawk is a cut above the others.

A Dealership Named Dankel and a Girl Named Cyndee

Hampton, Georgia

Don Hawk is amazed.

He's seen pit crews move fast before . . . but never this fast.

Trailing Terry Labonte by a full second more than three-quarters of the way through the 328-lap Puralator 500 at Atlanta Motor Speedway, Dale Earnhardt pulls his Monte Carlo onto pit road needing four tires and two cans of gas. The guys in the pit crew move like the proverbial greased lighting and get Earnhardt back on the track in only 19.72 seconds.

Labonte comes into the pit after the next lap, spending 21.81 seconds there. By the time he gets back on the track and up to racing speed, Earnhardt is in the lead by nearly 2 seconds. He never looks back and crosses the finish line comfortably ahead of Labonte for his second victory of the Winston Cup season. Earnhardt finishes the day with an average speed of 161.298

29

miles per hour, easily breaking the course record of 156.849 he had established six years earlier.

Knowing the victory was aided by the speedy work of the pit crew puts a satisfied smile on Don Hawk's face.

"Teamwork," he says, "is so important. We're all working together, pulling together, reaching for the same goal."

Don knows you can't win NASCAR races without an excellent driver like Dale Earnhardt. But the best driver would have trouble winning without a good team behind him. Don also believes that part of a team's responsibility is to look for new and better ways to accomplish its goals. "If you keep doing the things you've always done, you'll keep getting the results you've always gotten. Change what you do and you change the result."

Those two principles—the importance of teamwork and the necessity of innovation—were instilled in Don by his parents and reinforced by his experiences when he went back to Dankel Chevrolet shortly after his return from Dallas.

The Golden Boy Comes Home

The dealership's management welcomed Don back, happy to have its "favorite son" working for Dankel full time. As for Don, any doubts he had about the sudden turn in direction his life had taken were quickly forgotten. He was reminded every day how much he loved working around cars.

To those who worked with him, it seemed as if Don had a turbine inside that wouldn't cool down. If he wasn't thinking about how to get more work into the service bays, he was trying to figure out ways to do the work they already had better and more efficiently. He had ideas on just about everything at the dealership, including how to improve interaction with customers, parts suppliers, the sales team, and management.

He wasn't looking for glory for himself. He simply wanted to make Dankel Chevrolet the best dealership in town. For that reason, when he had what he thought was a good idea, he went straight to the person who was in a position to implement it.

He never thought that, due to his age, some people might resent his attitude, might think he was brash and cocky.

So it was that when Don hit upon a way to get more work through the service department in a shorter amount of time—and thereby make more money for the dealership—he decided to take it straight to the general manager. Seeing the door to the man's office was closed, he knocked and then walked in. The GM had someone else in his office—Don didn't know who—and seemed slightly annoyed by the interruption. He shot Don a look that seemed to say, "Whatever you want, make it quick."

"Do you need something?"

"Sorry to interrupt," Don said, "but I have something important I want to share with you. It won't take more than thirty seconds to explain it, but I have an idea for our service department that will make it run smoother, generate more money, and make more people happy."

The general manager stood up and gestured angrily in the direction of the door.

"When I want your opinion about the car business, or anything else for that matter, I'll ask for it."

Don started to protest, thought better of it, and quietly walked out of the office, gently closing the door. He was bruised by the encounter, but not defeated. He would just have to find someone who would listen. He knew his idea was good, even if he didn't have twenty-five years of experience in the auto industry.

Instead of being slowed by his boss's rebuff, he poured himself even more energetically into his job. And his work away from the dealership was just as busy. Don had taken the position of youth pastor at his home church and directed activities at the Allentown Boys' Home, where he had taken up residence. Life at the home was particularly stressful because the staff never knew when one of the boys would get sick in the middle of the night or some other emergency might arise. It wasn't Don's job to attend to middle-of-the-night emergencies, but here, as everywhere else, he worked full-bore. If he saw a way he could be of service, he moved into it.

31

The Girl Next Door

The frenzied schedule wasn't anything new to Don. He had become a master at squeezing every last second out of each day, so he pressed the accelerator harder and revved his engines a bit closer to the red line. Moving at a speed that reminded some of the Roadrunner of cartoon fame, he exploded in and out of his roles at church, Dankel, and the boys' home at a pace that blurred days into weeks and almost caused him not to notice the girl next door. He didn't miss her, though, and for that he will be forever grateful.

"I think it was a Sunday morning," he says, smiling at the memory. "I crawled into a pair of painter's pants to take the dog out. I was barefoot, unshaven, no shirt, looking just as rumpled as the pants I had on—the perfect model for a shaving cream or shampoo commercial."

Don figured it was safe to dress that way because it was early in the morning and the boys at the home were still asleep.

That's when he saw her. She was sweeping the sidewalk in back of the girls' home a few doors down. And she was beautiful.

Her name was Cyndee.

"I hadn't seen her until that very moment, which was truly strange, because she had been there for three months."

What Don didn't know was that even though he had never noticed her, she had seen him. Actually, she had heard about him even before getting her first glimpse of him.

Cyndee had been praying for several years that God would bring into her life a godly, Christian man who would become her husband. At age twenty-seven, she was not overly anxious to be married, yet she was beginning to wonder when God was going to answer that prayer.

That's why she took notice when some women from the neighborhood who were visiting the girls' home asked if she knew about the new youth minister who was working at the boys' home. She hadn't heard about him, but the moment she did, something began to stir deep inside her heart.

Looking back on it now, she says, "There have only been a few times in my life when I've really felt like I heard God speak to me, and this was one of them. It was just so clear to me that this would be my future husband, and I'm not an easy person to persuade. I felt like I must have been blushing because of the realization that came over me."

If her visitors noticed Cyndee's strange reaction to their question, they didn't let on. But Cyndee was so moved by the experience that she half expected Don to come to her door the following morning with a big bouquet of flowers. Instead, days went by without so much as a glimpse of her future husband. She remembers peeking through the blinds at him one day because the assurance from God was so strong that he was "the one."

"I was thinking, 'Well, if I'm going to marry him, let me at least see what he looks like,'" she recalls with a laugh.

Finally, she decided to sweep the sidewalk on that Sunday morning—pretend to sweep was more like it—because Don was outside and it seemed to be a matter of "now or never." She already had given the girls' home notice that she was leaving, and she didn't want to take the chance of missing out on God's best for her life. She knew that if it was God's will for the two of them to be together, it could happen even if she left that day without getting the chance to meet Don. On the other hand, maybe God wanted her to act on the knowledge he had given her, so that's what she did.

When Don saw Cyndee sweeping the sidewalk, he was instantly attracted to her. Once he talked to her, he also began to feel the stirring in his soul. He didn't know he had met the young woman he was going to marry, but he certainly knew there was something special about her.

Don says he figured it was just his luck that the day he first encountered Cyndee he looked "like the poster boy for some help-the-homeless organization."

It didn't seem to matter to Cyndee. She smiled and talked to him politely while continuing her sweeping. She told him she was finishing her duties at the girls' home that day and heading home to New Jersey.

"I couldn't believe my horrible timing," Don says. "I finally meet a very attractive young woman who was right under my nose all those months, and the day I meet her she's leaving for home. I wanted to ask her if she couldn't please stay a few more days, but I knew my appearance wouldn't help that argument too much."

Then opportunity knocked. Or as Don says, "The Lord gave me a window of opportunity." Cyndee was having car trouble and wondered if it was serious enough to prevent her from leaving. Don volunteered to look at her car, and he saw quickly that with a minor adjustment to the water pump belt, he could have it running perfectly. He fought off the temptation to tell her it might be best to delay her trip.

"I wish I could tell you it'll be at least Wednesday before I can have your car running, because that would give me a little more time to get to know you. But the truth is, I can fix the problem in an hour."

It was the right thing to say. Although Cyndee did leave that day, she and Don began writing to each other and dating when they could. A few weeks later, they traveled together to her sister's home in New York. As they headed up I-95, their young relationship passed its first serious test.

They were talking about things they liked and didn't like when Cyndee started fiddling with the radio knob.

"What are you looking for?" he asked. "Can I help you find it?"

"I'm trying to see if I can get a country station," came her reply.

"Country!" Don almost slammed on the brakes. He hated country music.

"You've got to be kidding me!"

"Why? What do you mean?" Her perplexed look showed she wasn't kidding.

"You really like country music?" Don asked.

"Yeah. I love it."

"Man alive," Don exclaimed. "If there's one thing I don't do, it's country music."

Cyndee wasn't about to be moved from her position.

"Well, what kind of music do you like?"

Don rattled off the names of some of his favorite musical groups, and Cyndee said calmly, "Well if you like those people, you'll probably like country music. At least give it a try."

By that time, Cyndee had found a country music station, and Don agreed to listen—at least for a while. He wasn't crazy about most of the music but figured if this was the only thing about Cyndee that bothered him, it was a small price to pay.

They drove for a while without speaking, listening to the sounds of Linda Ronstadt and Alabama. When a song came on that Cyndee particularly liked, she shook her head and said teasingly, "I can't believe you don't like country music."

"Well," Don said, "there must be something you don't like."

Cyndee thought for a moment. "Yes, I guess so," she finally said.

"Well, tell me about it. What is the one thing in all the world that you dislike the most?"

"I guess it would have to be . . . car racing."

"Car racing!" Don shouted. Then he added for the second time in about ten miles, "You've got to be kidding me!"

Cyndee didn't know that Don owned a race car and that it was sitting in his garage back home. Next to God, racing had always been his passion, and she was saying it was the one thing she didn't like.

"This is not good," he thought. "This is really not good. What in the world am I going to do?"

He looked into Cyndee's cool blue eyes, and what he saw there made him forget for a moment about racing. She was so pretty—slim and attractive, with her ash-blonde hair framing her perfect face and smile. He almost forgot he was driving. If he had to give up racing to keep this beautiful woman in his life, then it was good-bye racing.

As it turned out, Don sold his race car several weeks later and eventually came to like country music almost as much as Cyndee does. Cyndee has learned that there is something to be said for the sounds, sights, smells, and excitement of NASCAR racing.

Shortly after that trip, Don proposed and Cyndee accepted. They were married a few months later. That same year, Don accepted a new job at Drew Chevrolet in Elizabeth, New Jersey. It was nearly a ninety-minute commute each way from their home in the city of Freehold, but Don figured the time spent on the road was worth it. The dealership was large and wanted to hire Don as the assistant service manager. An older, very quiet, disciplined man named Mike Kalinak was Don's boss. Kalinak quickly became a sort of father figure to Don, and instead of being threatened by or jealous of his aggressive young assistant, took the time to pass on everything he knew about running the service department—which was plenty.

Kalinak was an honest man who never took advantage of customers, and Don appreciated his obvious integrity. He knew how hard it could be to maintain absolute honesty in a highly competitive business with a reputation for profiting from unscrupulous treatment of customers.

Hard Work Pays Off

Eight months into his stint at Drew Chevrolet, Don received an object lesson he has never forgotten. An elderly man Don knew only as Mr. Gutterlade invited him to his upstairs office at the dealership, saying, "I want to show you something."

Gutterlade always seemed to have an unlit cigar in his mouth, and that's pretty much all Don knew about him. He didn't know that Gutterlade had loaned Victor Potamkin, owner of the largest auto dealership in the world, the money that got him started in the business. The older man took Don over to the small wall safe in his office and asked him to turn around so he couldn't see the combination. Don stood with his back to the wall, listening to a series of clicks as Gutterlade turned the knob. When Don received permission to turn around, he saw that Gutterlade held a stack of certificates of deposit, each worth ten thousand dollars. The older man fanned the certificates in his hand so Don could get a good look at them.

"Son," he said, "you have the ability to go far in the car business if you treat it the way you do now. Keep working as hard as you are, and you'll have a stack of these for yourself by the time you're done."

Don was impressed by the sight of all that money. But he had never been motivated solely by the desire for wealth. It meant more to him that his efforts were being recognized. And it was good to be reminded that hard, honest work would pay off. He would need to remember that lesson in the near future.

"Thank you, sir," Don said politely.

Gutterlade turned, put the money back in the safe, closed the door, and gave the lock a whirl. Then the old man and the young assistant service manager walked back downstairs together.

France on Hawk

Bill France, president, NASCAR: Don has done a good job for Dale Earnhardt, and at the same time he recognizes that the sport needs to move right along, because Dale's going to move along with it. In other words, he's got a good, long-term view of things, versus just trying to do something to turn a quick buck on a short-term basis.

There are a lot of people in this world who aren't focused when they first get out of bed in the morning. Don is one of those individuals who gets up sharp, hits the ground running, and knows where he's going.

I believe that he and Dale Earnhardt complement each other perfectly. Dale's primary focus is out on that racetrack. He has to be focused and occupied in that area. Since there's only twenty-four hours in a day and seven days in a week, somebody has got to take care of the other activities, and Don is doing a good job of that.

He knows that, as good a driver as Dale Earnhardt is, nobody is going to want to buy a ticket to see him drive if he doesn't have anyone to race against. Because of that, the business moves he makes are designed not just to benefit the Earnhardt-Childress team, but all of NASCAR as well.

I've never heard anybody put a knock on him.

The High Price of Integrity

Bristol, Tennessee

It is the kind of day you almost expect to see a strange-looking boat float by full of two of every kind of animal.

It is raining, and raining hard.

NASCAR officials have done their best to run the Food City 500, finally giving up after 342 laps on the half-mile banked Bristol Motor Speedway. Jeff Gordon was well ahead of the pack and, after a sixty-seven-minute delay, he is declared the winner.

This race is probably the easiest race Gordon has ever won. He has spent most of his time chatting with friends and watching the radar screen to see if the rain would let up. But he isn't very happy about the way things turned out.

"I hated to see it end like that. The car was at its best right when the rain started to come down. We were about to lap some pretty strong cars."

By the time the race was officially declared over, the grandstands were almost deserted, even the most dedicated fans having fled long before to higher ground.

"I've never won a race like this before," Gordon reflects. "To be in victory lane without a soul in the grandstand and pouring down rain was really weird."

Gordon took the lead from Rusty Wallace on lap 295 and stayed in front until the rain made it impossible to continue. Terry Labonte finished in second position, followed by Mark Martin, Dale Earnhardt, Wallace, and Dale Jarrett. Don Hawk is convinced that Earnhardt was still in good position to challenge for the lead, but there's simply nothing you can do when Mother Nature won't cooperate. All Earnhardt can do is go home and wait for a better day.

As for Don, he's been through enough storms in his life that he's not disturbed by a little rain, or even rain that comes down in torrents as it is right now here on the Tennessee-Virginia border.

Stepping into the Storm

Today, Don is thinking in particular of some stormy weather that came his way in the years immediately after he left his job at Drew Chevrolet.

He'd been at Drew for two years, was comfortable enough there, and was making a good salary. A couple could do just great on what he was making, but Don wasn't so sure about a family.

He was especially anxious to find a better job after Cyndee became pregnant. She had a difficult pregnancy and was hospitalized a couple of times. During one of the hospital stays, a nurse said to her, "I don't know why they're putting you through this, because you'll never carry this baby." The cruel words sliced deeply into Cyndee's heart, and she began to cry.

But even before the first tears had rolled down her cheeks, Cyndee felt God was talking to her, telling her that her unborn child was going to be all right. That was the second time in her life that Cyndee was certain God was speaking to her, and again he honored his word. Jessica was born at full-term, completely healthy, and normal in every way.

About this time Don contacted some people at Chevrolet and asked if they knew of any opportunities. They told him about a dealership in New Jersey recently purchased by a group that owned several other businesses. The dealership needed someone to run its parts and service operation. The situation sounded just right for him, so Don called and asked for an interview. He was offered the job.

To his dismay, Don found that things there weren't run with the integrity he had come to expect at the Dankel and Drew dealerships. When he was hired, the company agreed to pay him a salary plus performance incentives. Then it shortchanged him on his first bonus check. Because Don kept his own ledgers, he knew immediately that the dealership's figures were wrong.

Normally, Don didn't even open his pay envelopes. He gave them to Cyndee, who deposited his checks in the bank. Because this was a first bonus check from a new dealer, he decided to open the envelope himself. But first he drove home so Cyndee could share in the excitement of receiving what was sure to be a substantial bonus.

His jaw dropped when he saw that the figure on the check wasn't even close to what it should have been.

"Something's wrong here! I'm going right back down there and talk to the owner about this."

Cyndee put her hand on his arm.

"I don't know, Don. Are you sure you want to do that?"

Don was sure. Perhaps it was an honest mistake. Such things did happen. But if it was something intentional . . . well, Don wasn't about to work for a company that didn't demonstrate absolute integrity. And so, despite Cyndee's misgivings, he strode out the door, hopped into the family car, and drove straight back to the dealership.

The owner was in his office, poring over some paperwork when Don walked in.

"Hi, Don, what's up? You need something?"

"Yes, as a matter of fact, I do. I think there's been a mistake made on this check."

He was trying to give his boss the benefit of the doubt.

41

He pushed the check onto the desk in front of the man, who looked at it, shrugged, and said, "No, I don't think so. Looks right to me."

Don calmly went back over the agreement he had made with the company when he was hired, just to make sure they both saw it the same way.

"Yes, that's right," the owner replied. "And based on that agreement, this is exactly what we owe you."

"No," Don said, firmly, "that's not true. I may be a bit of a crazy man, but I keep my own ledgers. I know how much we've made in service since I began, and our figures don't agree."

The owner gave Don a patronizing smile and shook his head, holding out the check as if to say, "You'd better take it, because it's all you're going to get."

Don wasn't having any of it, and his blood pressure was quickly approaching the boiling point.

"Listen," he said. "If you're going to play with the tax man, play with the tax man. If you're going to play with Chevrolet, play with Chevrolet. But don't play games with my life."

He wasn't trying to be flippant or smart-alecky. He treated people honestly and expected to be treated the same way.

"Don't talk to me like that," snarled the owner, flipping the check back in Don's direction. "If you don't like it here, you can leave."

Don's response had been formulated in his mind even before the conversation began.

"Well, that's basically what I came back to tell you. Because if we don't get along on our first check, and if you're not going to admit your mistake or at least look into the problem, then I'm gone."

He turned on his heel and walked out of the dealership into the night air, unemployed for the first time since high school.

Don wasn't at all frightened, because he knew he had done the right thing and believed that God would honor it. He had no doubt that he'd find another position quickly, and he was right. Don saw that a multicar franchise in Pennsylvania was advertising for a service manager, applied for the position, and immediately received an interview.

Searching for an Honest Man

During the interview, one of the men kept slipping out of the room, although Don had no idea why. It wasn't until later that he found out what was going on: While he was being questioned, Cyndee was being asked the same questions out in the lot, where she was waiting for the interview to end. The owners were checking Don's answers against Cyndee's answers to make sure they were dealing with an honest man.

Some men might have been irritated or insulted by that apparent lack of trust, but Don appreciated it. It showed him they wanted to hire an honest man, which he took to mean they were honest men themselves. After the way his previous job had ended, Don desperately wanted to work for a company that demonstrated integrity in all its dealings.

Don was offered the job and accepted immediately. He looks back on that decision as one of the best he ever made, because it allowed him to become a student of Peter Criscuolo, who was the head of the parts and service departments of all the organization's dealerships.

Don believes Criscuolo was the best parts and service man in America. He respected Criscuolo so much that he sat down and listened without a word of protest when Criscuolo told him one day, "You have a big battery. If you listen to me and shut up, you're gonna be good."

Together, the two of them were good. They drove the dealership's service department to the point where, in some months, profits exceeded those from new car sales. Everything seemed to be going great. The dealership was growing, Don was turning into an excellent service manager, and he thoroughly enjoyed his relationship with Criscuolo, who was not only a teacher and colleague but a friend.

Naturally, Don was disappointed when Criscuolo announced he was leaving to take a position with a company based in Wilmington, Delaware. But even though Don hated to see his friend and mentor leave, he was encouraged when Criscuolo expressed complete confidence in him, telling him that he knew Don was more than capable of doing the job both of them had been doing together. Then, Criscuolo reminded his young friend that life is a series of cycles and said some day they would link up again.

Don didn't realize Criscuolo was already thinking about that day as he said good-bye. Nor did he know that his mentor would be watching to see how far Don could fly on his own before they joined forces again.

There would be some rough flying before that happened.

The Fall Guy

For a few years after Criscuolo's departure, everything went well for Don. The parts and service department continued to grow and prosper under his management.

Then word came that Chevrolet was going to conduct a warranty review at the dealership. The owner, general manager, and Don were summoned to meet with representatives from corporate headquarters to explain overcharges and other questionable practices in warranty operations.

Don was astounded as he listened to the charges being leveled against his service department. He was especially surprised when the Chevrolet representatives wanted to know why there was a seventeen-thousand-dollar charge-back to their company for certain warranty work. The repair orders were pulled and laid out on a table in front of Don. One order was for a new engine which was put into a truck with 117,000 miles on it. The manufacturer wanted to know how this work could have been approved for a truck that was so far past its warranty protection. When Don looked at the work order, he saw that the engine had been put into a truck owned by the father-in-law of the dealership's general manager. He didn't want to start accusing anyone, so all he could say to the Chevrolet representative was, "That's not my handwriting or my signature on the work order."

As a result of the warranty review, Chevrolet put the dealership on probation for a year. The manufacturer also asked for a written proposal describing how such gross mismanagement would be prevented in the future.

At his first opportunity, Don went to see the dealership's general manager. The man fidgeted and squirmed from the moment Don walked into his office, and when Don suggested there was something wrong, he exploded.

"Yeah, you're right!" he shouted. "There is something wrong here and you're responsible!"

Before Don could utter a word in his own defense, the man continued, "As a matter of fact, if you don't resign right now, we're going to sue you."

"Sue me? For what?"

"For defamation of character."

"Defamation of—"

"That's right! Defamation of character. After all, you're responsible for the service department. Whether or not you're personally responsible doesn't matter. All of these things happened on your watch, and then you defamed the owner's character to save your own hide. I want your resignation on my desk first thing tomorrow morning. If I don't have it, we'll sue you."

Don tried to reason with the man, but it was no use. Most of the work in question was done on a truck owned by the general manager's father-in-law. How could the man not know that? Of course he knew.

After his stormy confrontation with the general manager, Don returned to his office and began digging through the files. He discovered that other repair orders for the general manager's relatives also were charged to Chevrolet. So were repairs and other services for members of the owner's family. Even worse, the factory representative from Chevrolet had work done on a car in Don's service department, and that bill was charged to Chevrolet.

Unsure of the best course of action, Don called his old friend, Peter Criscuolo. He laid out the whole scheme, and Criscuolo said, "You need to get out of there fast. But you can't leave with them winning and Chevrolet thinking you did something unethical."

"Yeah, that's what I thought."

"Call your dad and see if he can get you a good lawyer. Then go down there and meet them head-on."

Don called his father, who was a nationally known tax advisor and well-connected in the business community.

His father's advice was quick and to the point.

"You call your boss in and tell him the shoe is on the wrong foot. Tell him you're the one who's going to sue. Him, his company, everybody who's involved in this thing."

After talking to his father, Don walked back down to the general manager's office and asked him to summon the owner.

"No way. He has nothing to say to you."

"Either he talks to me now," Don replied, "or he'll be talking to my father and our legal counsel."

The general manager changed his mind. He buzzed the owner on the intercom and urged him to come down, "right now."

The owner went on the attack the moment he walked into the room. "Look! You think you got something to bring against me, then bring it on."

Don shrugged. If that was what the man wanted. "I'm not going to let you get away with making me the fall guy in your warranty scam," he said. "If this is what you want, we can both go public. You tell your story and I'll tell mine."

The owner waved his hand in a dismissive gesture. "You're full of it," he sneered. "No one's going to take your word over mine."

"Oh, they won't have to take my word for it," Don smiled. "You have a lot of dealerships, and those dealerships have their own service departments, run by other service managers. I'm sure that what's going on here is going on in those other departments as well. All I have to do is do a little digging and Chevrolet will realize who's really trying to beat them—and it won't be Don Hawk."

He paused to let his words sink in, and then added, "I'm not going down easy."

There was an awkward silence. The general manager sat behind his desk, staring at the floor. The owner paced back and forth, contemplating his next move. He was trapped and he knew it.

Finally, he said in a conciliatory tone, "Listen, there's no reason we have to drag this into court. Why don't we see if we can find a solution that works for all of us?"

He started by offering Don two weeks of paid vacation in which to look for another job.

No deal.

Don insisted upon a written statement from the dealership explaining the real reason he was leaving. He also wanted to know how the owner was going to take care of medical coverage for Don's growing family and what he was going to offer in addition to the two weeks of vacation time Don already had coming to him.

The owner shot a questioning look in the general manager's direction and then asked Don to leave the office for a few minutes. When Don returned, he was told he would be given six weeks of severance pay and eight weeks of medical coverage for his family, with an option for an additional month if he hadn't found a job in that time. He was also told that he could keep his company car for two months or until he found a job, whichever came first.

Don didn't like it very much. After all, he hadn't done anything unethical or illegal. But he didn't like working for people who had. So he agreed to what they were offering and then drove home and told Cyndee it was time to start looking for another job.

Nemechek on Hawk

Andrea Nemechek, owner of Bell South Corporation car #42, which her husband, Joe, drives: Don's a very good Christian man and a good businessman. He's always been there for Joe and me when we've needed help. It's been a big step to jump from Busch Series to Winston Cup racing, and Joe has always needed somebody to talk to. Dale Earnhardt was the first one Joe really got a chance to know. Then Don came along, and both of them have helped Joe through rough times and advised him about decisions he was making.

Don cares about people. He also takes part in chapel services all the time, and he's touched a lot of people through what he's said and done there . . . the teaching that he's done.

I think Don kind of calms Dale Earnhardt down, saves him and protects him from things that might be a problem for him. They're two very dissimilar people, and that's probably part of what makes them so good together.

Don's personality and his Christian experience are good for the NASCAR family. He's just an alive person, and I don't think there's anybody in the garage area who can say they don't like Don Hawk.

Now, if we could have him come to work for us and make us as successful as Dale Earnhardt, that would be great!

"Do Whatever You Have to Do to Hire That Guy"

Martinsville, Virginia

Every driver on the Winston Cup circuit knows the pain that can result from a simple mechanical failure. When your car lets you down, there's nothing you can do except sit and watch the other drivers zip past you.

Today at Martinsville Speedway in the Goody's Headache Powders 500, it is Terry Labonte's turn to feel that pain.

And what makes it worse for Labonte is that it should have been his day. He was setting a record by driving in his 514th consecutive Winston Cup event, a streak that went back to the opening race of the 1979 season—an amazing achievement in a sport so conducive to injury. Labonte was breaking the mark set by legendary NASCAR driver Richard Petty, the man still regarded by many fans as the king of stock car racing.

For most of the race at Martinsville, it looked as if Labonte was going to add to his achievement by capturing the checkered flag. He was leading as late as the 414th lap in the 500-lap event before he was done in by a brake fluid leak. Over the last

49

86 laps, he was forced into the pit several times and wound up in 24th place, 20 laps back of eventual winner Rusty Wallace.

Wallace, NASCAR's leading driver on tracks shorter than one mile in length, passed Jeff Gordon with 12 laps to go on the half-mile oval, and raced to the 42nd victory of his career. The victory was also his 6th at Martinsville and his 1st of the Winston Cup season. Wallace's day wasn't without difficulties. Mechanical problems forced him into the pits several times in the middle of the race, but his crew soon had his car back in perfect running order, and he breezed the rest of the way home.

Although Earnhardt challenged for the lead in the early going, he had fallen back into the middle of the pack by the end of the race. But he knows, as does his business manager, that one race does not a season make. There will be other Sundays on other tracks in which to prove their team is a winner—the best of the best.

The Truth Will Set You Free

That was exactly how Don Hawk felt after his warranty showdown. His bosses had tried to make him the scapegoat, painting him as a loser who had been dishonest in an effort to line his own pockets. Despite their accusations, Don was able to leave with his head held high because he knew the truth, and he believed that, as the Bible says, the truth will set you free. No matter what they might say about him, others would come to see that he was a man of integrity. It wasn't so important whether he won or lost in the fight against his unscrupulous bosses. What mattered most to Don was that he proved himself to be a winner in the game of life.

Within twenty-four hours of becoming unemployed, Don saw two newspaper ads placed by Kerbeck Cadillac in Palmyra, New Jersey, a suburb of Camden. The world's largest Cadillac dealer was looking for a general sales manager and a service manager.

It seemed to Don that somebody upstairs was looking out for him. Even though the nation's economy wasn't exactly booming at the time and unemployment was high, there was always an opening perfectly suited to Don's abilities. Because his most recent experience as a service manager hadn't worked out so well, Don thought it might be time to try something else. He applied for the sales manager position. But when he was interviewed by the general manager, he learned that the most important thing for the owner, Frank Kerbeck, was finding someone who could fix major problems in the service department. Don seemed supremely qualified to do just that, but before he agreed to anything, he wanted the Kerbeck people to understand the conditions under which he had left his previous employer.

Don tried to tell the story in a calm, straightforward manner. He didn't want to come across as if he were full of sour grapes, but he also wanted the general manager to understand that he wasn't about to return to that type of situation.

The general manager asked Don to wait in another room while he made a couple of phone calls. Afterward, he politely told Don that everything looked good and invited him to come back that afternoon to meet Frank Kerbeck. The man was polite, but he wasn't particularly enthusiastic, and Don figured he was being given the brush-off. On the drive home, he decided not to go back that afternoon. After all, he still had all that severance pay, so he didn't need to find a new job right away.

Cyndee took a different view of the situation.

"It wouldn't hurt to go down there and see if he was telling the truth," she advised. "Maybe they're more interested in you than you think."

After Don thought about it for a while, he decided she was right.

That afternoon he drove back to Kerbeck for an interview with the owner—an interview he never really expected to take place.

Kerbeck Cadillac was a plush, elegant operation. With massive sixteen-foot plateglass windows, Corinthian pillars, and marble fountains out front, it could have been mistaken for a vacation resort. A customer almost could expect to see a doorman in uniform allowing people in and out of the showroom. Don noticed as he pulled up in front of the dealership that the owner's two parking spaces were filled by luxury automobiles—a Lamborghini Countach and a Ferrari. If those cars were any indication, the man's business was doing very well, indeed.

To Don's surprise, the receptionist told him that not only was Kerbeck expecting him but he was waiting for him in his office. Don had another surprise when he got there: Kerbeck was about Don's age—young to be running such a successful business. Before their conversation was through, Kerbeck had offered Don a generous starting salary, a new Cadillac to drive, and a substantial bonus if he would build up the service department here the way he had done for his previous employer.

On the Nightshift

Don appreciated the generous offer and looked forward to meeting the challenge. Not so exciting, however, were the conditions. Kerbeck wanted Don to start a new service operation that would be open from four in the afternoon until midnight. The dealership's normal hours were from eight to five, and during that time the regular service department handled all the work.

Furthermore, Don was to build his service operation from the ground up. No one from the daytime operation would be transferred to his team—no mechanics, no service managers, nobody. He had to hire all his personnel and train them in his system, so that's what he did.

Still, within eight months, the nightshift was billing more than the day crew. Kerbeck was so pleased he placed Don in charge of both shifts. And a few months later, the owner presented Don with another challenge. He told him he wanted a Rolls Royce franchise. To get it he would have to modify his service department and showroom to meet Rolls Royce's impeccable standards. The entire service area and the showroom would have to be painted white, a color chosen by Rolls Royce because its cars show so well against a white background.

"Do you think you can handle that, Don?" Kerbeck asked.

"Sure," Don shrugged. "No problem."

"Well, actually, there is one problem," Kerbeck said.

"Which is?"

"It has to be done within twenty-four hours."

"What?" Don gasped. "You've got to be kidding!"

"No, Don, I'm not kidding. They'll be here tomorrow right around this time."

Don looked at his watch and saw that it was just after one in the afternoon.

"I know you can do it, Don," Kerbeck said. "I don't know anybody else who could, but I'm sure you can."

Don only had a minute to think about the impossibility of the task. How was he going to find enough people to do all the painting? How was he going to find the necessary hundreds of gallons of white paint? And how could he possibly get it dry in time?

Don solved the first problem by asking all his mechanics to call any of their friends who might be available to help. Then he went to the unemployment office and hired several people right off the benefit lines. He needed an army to paint the shop walls, floors, and showroom, and he put one together quickly.

The second problem wasn't quite so easy to deal with, but after calling just about every paint dealer in the Camden area, he was able to get enough white paint to do the job.

Later that evening, when Kerbeck came by the dealership to see how the work was going, he found Don painting alongside his men. His tie was down around his waist, and white paint was splattered all over his hair, face, and suit.

"I knew you could do it!" Kerbeck called out.

"We're trying," was all the exhausted Hawk could say.

"Yeah, but it looks like you've ruined your suit."

Don stopped working and glanced down at the paint splattered all over his slacks. "So it would appear," he said.

Kerbeck told Don that as soon as the work was over and the Rolls Royce team had come and gone, he would turn Don's ruined clothes into three new Armani suits. All Don had to do was pick them out of a closet in Kerbeck's home.

By 2:30 in the morning, all the painting was done and about 60 percent dry. Kerbeck returned and, although he was amazed that the painting had been finished, he was upset because he believed the walls would never dry in time for the inspection. Even if they did, the smell of fresh paint would be noticeable for days.

As politely as he could, Don told the boss to go home and stop worrying. Once Kerbeck left, Don brought all of the body shop heaters into the showroom and turned every exhaust fan in the dealership on high to suck out the paint smell.

By 5:30, the fans were turned off and the heaters returned to the body shop. Walls and floors were a bright, pristine white. They were dry. And there wasn't even a hint of new paint smell. When Kerbeck arrived at the dealership that morning, he loved what he saw. So did the Rolls Royce inspection team. Kerbeck got the Rolls Royce franchise he wanted. Although Don refused the offer of Armani suits, his boss placed a roll of bills into his pocket and told him to use the money for his kids.

Again, life was getting comfortable for Don and Cyndee Hawk and their growing family. Don had built the Kerbeck service department into an extremely profitable twenty-four-hours-a-day operation, was earning a nice income, and driving a new Cadillac Brougham. All the signs were there. His life was about to take another turn.

A Voice from the Past

This time, the change came in the form of a telephone call from Peter Criscuolo. It had been three years since the two of them had worked together, but Criscuolo had kept track of his student's progress. All he told Don when he called was that they were going to fly together again, and that he would pick him up at the drive-in theater across the street from Kerbeck Cadillac the following afternoon.

Until then, Hawk had never missed a full day of work in his life. But now, because of one phone call out of the blue from Peter Criscuolo, he was going to use his first sick day, and he didn't even know why. All he knew was that he trusted and respected Criscuolo, and if he said it was important, then it must be important.

Don knew his old friend had been working with the Winner group of dealerships in Delaware and New Jersey, and he figured they would be driving to the big Winner dealership in Cherry Hill, New Jersey. They didn't. Instead, they headed south to Newark, Delaware, and a Winner Ford dealership so small that showroom, service department, and all, could fit into a corner of the department he was running at Kerbeck Cadillac. Not only that, but it was obvious that it hadn't had a new paint job in . . . well, probably since the building was constructed.

When they parked across the street from the building, Don thought for a moment that perhaps Criscuolo was teasing him. The two of them were going to have a good laugh and then drive on to their real destination. But when Don looked at Criscuolo's face, he saw that this was no joke.

"That's it," Criscuolo said. "That's you and me. We're going to turn it into the best service area in the country. But you have to understand before we go in that the general manager is a bear. You've never met anybody tougher, crazier, or harder to get along with. I don't think he even likes his own mother."

Hawk still couldn't believe what he was seeing. Why should he give up Kerbeck's massive showroom with all its magnificent glass and water fountain out front for something that looked like it came out of *Mad* magazine?

At Kerbeck, oil and grease spills had to be wiped clean and dried with a cloth immediately. This dealership apparently didn't know that oil spills were ugly, dirty, and dangerous. It was obvious that nobody had even tried to clean them up.

When Don got over his astonishment enough to speak, he asked about mechanics, parts people, service writers, and service managers. The answers did not make him feel any better. The dealership had five mechanics, three parts people, and one guy who doubled as a service writer and service manager.

"Well," Don said, "I guess we'd better go on in." He started to open his door, but Criscuolo stopped him.

"No. Not yet. We've got to wait for a few more minutes."

"Wait? Why."

Criscuolo looked at his watch, "Because it's not 5:30 yet."

"Five-thirty? What does that have to do with it?"

"That's when the service manager leaves. If we come in while he's still here, he'll get mad and quit."

This was getting more ridiculous to Don all the time, but he had come this far, so he figured he might as well see it through. And so, a little past 5:30, they drove into the service area of the dealership. It was one lane in, a ninety-degree right turn, and one lane out. Don didn't tell his old friend what he was thinking, but the words echoing through his mind were "rat hole."

In the showroom, Criscuolo introduced Hawk to A. J., the general manager of the dealership, and the burly man told him to wait while he talked to Criscuolo in private. All Don could think as he stood alone in the showroom was, "What in the world am I doing here?" And he couldn't help wondering if his old friend hadn't lost at least one or two of his marbles over the past three years.

After a few minutes, A. J. and Criscuolo came back out, and the general manager said he was ready to meet with Don alone in his office. As soon as they were seated, A. J. told Don he didn't want anyone coming in and changing things around in his service department. He liked things just the way they were. Criscuolo could change Winner's other dealerships any way he wanted, but not here.

Having made that clear, A. J. leaned back in his chair and asked Don why he wanted to leave his job at Kerbeck.

Don almost laughed in spite of himself.

"I have no intention of leaving Kerbeck," he answered. "I'm only here as a courtesy to Peter."

A. J. sat up straight, surprised by Don's honest response.

"Well . . ." he sputtered, "why do you think Peter brought you here?"

"That's easy," Don replied. "He wants to turn your service department into the best service operation in the country, and he wants me to help him do it."

That was pretty much the gist of their conversation. A. J. stood up, shook Don's hand, thanked him for coming, and asked him to send Criscuolo back into his office. Within ten minutes, the two were back in Criscuolo's car, heading up I-95 toward New Jersey.

Don was thinking, "Well, it didn't take him long to show us the door." He wasn't feeling unhappy about it. In fact, he was glad they had been able to get out of there so quickly. Still, the idea of teaming up once again with his old friend and mentor had been very appealing.

The two men drove along for a few minutes before Criscuolo broke the silence.

"I don't know what you told him in there, Hawk, but I've never seen A. J. so positive about anybody. His exact words to me were, 'Do whatever you have to do to hire that guy.'"

Don was surprised and gratified, and he promised his old friend he would think about it. But there were a lot of things he'd have to consider before making a move from Kerbeck Cadillac. During the next couple of weeks, Don kept reminding himself how good things were at Kerbeck, how comfortable he felt here. Furthermore, Kerbeck didn't want to lose Don and offered more money to convince him to stay. It should have been an easy decision in favor of staying put, but the decision Don was wrestling with had nothing to do with being comfortable or receiving more money. He was hearing a siren call to join up again with the man who had helped mold him into a top-notch service manager. And he was intrigued by the challenge of again trying to do the impossible—turning a tiny, run-down service department into one of the best in the country.

He also knew Criscuolo's words were true: "Take this place, turn it around, and the whole world will know who you are."

Getting Off to a Bad Start

Don finally decided to make the move to Winner Ford, and it only took him about one day to start wondering if he had made the right decision. By 7:30 in the evening, Don still had not been given his company car. He mentioned that fact to A. J., and in a few minutes the lot boy drove up in a used Ford Tempo with 44,000 miles on it and an engine that continued running for a few moments after the ignition was turned off. The Tempo had come off the "as is" line of cars the dealership unloaded at bargain prices.

Don drove the car home and almost made it back to work the next morning. It broke down about three miles from the dealership, forcing Don to walk the rest of the way. A. J. was in the showroom when Don walked in, and he asked pointedly if it was his service manager's custom to come to work late on his second full day.

Don's response was quick but restrained.

"Yes, it is my custom to arrive late when the company car assigned to me breaks down three miles from my office."

A. J. wasn't moved. "So? You're the service manager. Have it picked up and fix it."

Don was steaming inside, but he decided to do exactly what the general manager suggested. He knew he'd be having lunch in a week or so with Criscuolo and Dean O'Neill, a vice president with Ford, to discuss progress at Winner. When that day came, he insisted that they take his car, and the two men, who drove new Lincoln Town Cars, squeezed into Don's little Tempo.

O'Neill couldn't believe A. J. had given Don such a clunker to drive and asked him why he didn't make a fuss about it.

"Well," Don replied, "apparently this is what A. J. thinks I'm worth. So I'll drive it until I can prove to him I'm worth a whole lot more."

O'Neill wasn't so understanding, and when the men got back to the dealership, he told A. J. exactly how he felt.

At day's end, A. J. called Don into his office and threw him the keys to a new Ford LTD Brougham. "Here, crybaby," he said. "Your new company car."

Don immediately put the keys back on A. J.'s desk.

"I'm no crybaby," he said. "And I don't need an LTD to drive. I'll keep driving the Tempo until I've proven to you that I'm worth the LTD and you hand those keys to me instead of throwing them at me."

A. J. wasn't used to dealing with anyone who wouldn't meekly take what he dished out, and he was flustered. As Don turned to go, he called out after him, "Uh . . . wait a minute. What did you drive at Kerbeck?"

"What did I drive when I was at Kerbeck?"

"Yeah."

"You don't want to know."

A. J. followed Don out of the office and handed him the LTD keys. He knew he hadn't made a mistake on his new service manager. It was simply hard for him to accept change, and he wasn't sure he wanted it. Underneath it all, he understood how much his service department needed resurrection, and he was sure Don was the man to do the job. He was right.

Under Don's leadership, Winner Ford's roster of nine service employees grew to 101, and the service department work schedule expanded to twenty-four hours a day, seven days a week. For seven straight years Don's department won Ford's Distinguished Service Award, and Ford commissioned a film on the operation to show to other dealerships around the country. During that time Ford named Don its national service manager and began flying him to other dealerships so he could help them create a service department as good as the one they had built in Newark, Delaware.

Winner set Ford Motor Company records for quick lubes in a day, week, month, and year. In daily managers' meetings, Don went over what each department had done the day before and projected what they had to do that day to keep on track with their individual, department, and dealership goals.

Don believed then, as he does now, that teamwork and open communication are important ingredients of success. He wanted to make sure everyone knew exactly where the service department stood in relationship to its yearly objectives, and no one ever left those daily meetings without some motivational principle or slogan to help make the day a success.

Frank Kerbeck tried to lure Don back to his organization several times. Even though Don always politely turned him down, Kerbeck still brought him in occasionally to talk to his employees.

Following the Golden Rule

Every morning at Winner Ford, customers lined up outside the service department, each holding an appointment card just like the kind a dentist or doctor would give out with the appointment time written on it. When each customer's appointment time came, the name would be called out by the service writer or mechanic and the car would be taken in to be serviced. The way the system was set up, a customer never had to call to see if the work was completed or progressing on schedule. The Winner service department did the calling—twice. The first call was to let the customer know that work was progressing as promised, and the second was to say that servicing was done.

Don insisted that his mechanics be top-flight technicians who fixed cars right the first time. There weren't going to be any trumped-up charges on his watch. Neither were any important details to be done in a slipshod manner or left undone. He demanded complete integrity. It was important to him for customers to know that "if Winner Ford tells you something about your car, you can believe it." He wanted to ensure customer satisfaction and loyalty to his service department and the dealership. He knew that quality in his area not only increased the number of service customers for the dealership but boosted car sales as well.

He also knew that people who were treated fairly when their cars were being serviced were more likely to think of the dealership when it came time to buy new cars.

In this way, he was following the Golden Rule's admonition to treat others as you want them to treat you. He was also following the advice of Peter Criscuolo, who had told him, "The main problem in service departments in dealerships all over the country is that the people there don't treat their customers the way they'd want to be treated if they had brought their cars in for service."

Criscuolo had added, "If you keep doing the job you're doing without losing your integrity along the way, you'll make more money than you know what to do with."

60

So far, Don's experience was proving Criscuolo to be absolutely right.

But then, his life was about to take another turn, a turn leading right onto the high-banked ovals of the NASCAR circuit.

Estes on Hawk

Wayne Estes, media relations representative for Ford Motor Sports: Don Hawk is one of my best friends out here on the NASCAR circuit. I met him when he was at Winner Ford in Delaware, and most of his contacts with NASCAR really came through the Wood Brothers racing team when Winner Ford was doing business with them and with Alan Kulwicki. So Don is really a Ford guy in Chevy clothing.

When I met Don there were only six or seven Ford teams in Winston Cup, and when we went to Dover, Pocono, places like that, he was always there. Actually, he was at any track that was remotely close to where he worked in Newark, Delaware.

You look at Don and you know he just loves this life. It's very serious for him, yes, but he treats it like a game. He enjoys it like a kid in a candy store, or like a kid on a ball field, when he's working in the garage area on the weekend of a race. He just loves being a part of the whole deal. He gives it everything he's got, and just about everybody enjoys having him around.

The only thing is, if I could have my way, I'd have him wearing a blue Ford oval on his shirt.

A Season of Tragedy

Talladega, Alabama

It happened without warning.

One instant Dale Earnhardt was challenging for the lead at Talladega Superspeedway.

In the next, he had been hit and sent spinning out of control, directly into the path of several cars. Covering more than 150 feet of track every second, there was no way they could avoid him.

It came early, in the sixth lap, when all twelve cars were tightly bunched. It was over in seconds, but for Don Hawk, watching from the pit, it seemed much, much longer. His heart was in his throat as he saw Earnhardt's Number 3 lift into the air after being clipped from behind by Sterling Marlin.

Dust and smoke and pieces of bumpers and fenders flew in all directions. As the smoke hung in the air, paramedics and members of the pit crews sprinted onto the track to tend to the injured.

For now, Don knows that all he can do is stand back and pray that Earnhardt and everyone else involved in the accident will be okay. There have been tragedies before on this track. And losses that hit close to home.

Earnhardt is taken by ambulance to a local hospital, where doctors determine that he has broken his sternum and collarbone. He is in pain, but Don knows Earnhardt well enough to expect he won't let a few broken bones slow him for long. More than likely, he'll be ready to race by the next Winston Cup event, two weeks from today.

After witnessing Earnhardt's accident, Don doesn't really care so much who won. He is just happy that his friend and boss is alive and will be able to race another day. Don has seen too many tragedies—and lost too many friends—already.

Tragedy Is Never Far Away

Anyone who spends Sundays hurtling around the tight corners of a Winston Cup track at speeds approaching 200 miles per hour knows the danger of death is never far away. Every driver understands this—and every wife of every driver understands—even if nobody wants to admit it. A moment of inattention, a mechanical failure, a slight bump from a competitor, an unavoidable oil slick—any of those things is enough to send a car spinning out of control. And if it should hit the wall, there's not going to be much anyone can do except pick up the pieces and comfort the survivors.

Even though the threat of death is always present, it just isn't talked about. No one wants to acknowledge the possibility. If the specter is ignored, it just might go away.

Don is no stranger to the loss and tragedy that has always been a part of NASCAR racing. On this Sunday in Talladega, he can't help thinking of three race car drivers who are conspicuously absent: Alan Kulwicki, Davey Allison, and Neil Bonnett.

Kulwicki and Allison were killed during the 1993 Winston Cup season in air crashes. Both were considered to have great

Don Hawk strides down Pit Road.

A familiar sight: Dale Jarrett (#88) and Dale Earnhardt (#3), neck and neck. Jarrett won a hard-fought battle with Earnhardt in the Daytona 500. A week later Earnhardt took the lead from Jarrett to win the Goodwrench Service 400.

Don, hard at work in the pit.

Ernest Masche

Don Grassmann

(left) Don and Dale pose with the trophy after Dale won the Puralator 500 at Atlanta Motor Speedway. (above) Dale and Don deep in conversation. (below) Don Hawk and Teresa Earnhardt share a light moment at Dale's expense.

Don Grassmann

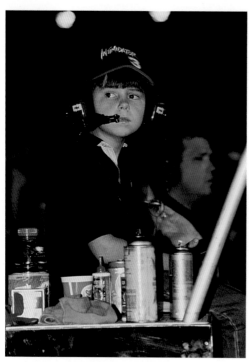

John Hawk takes in the racing action from his perch in the pit.

Jessica Hawk

Julie Hawk

Jenny Hawk

Don and Cyndee enjoy the Christmas party for Team 3 hosted by Richard Childress, owner of Dale's Monte Carlo.

Don's family joins him on race day at Pocono Raceway. From left: Don's mom, Harriet; his sisters, Sheila and Sharon; and his father, Don Sr.

Dale leads the field at Talladega Superspeedway. He would crash later in the race (inset).

Dale's pit crew works furiously to get him back in the race.

Terry Labonte, Jeff Gordon, Don, Dale, and Teresa relax at the Brickyard 400. Labonte and Gordon would finish the season first and second in the Winston Cup standings.

After nineteen seasons of chasing the Daytona 500 title, Dale finally wins the prize in 1998. A happy Don Hawk joins the Earnhardts—Dale, Teresa, and daughter Taylor Nicole—to pose with the trophy.

racing careers ahead of them when they died. Bonnett died in 1994 in a racing accident.

Kulwicki's death was particularly difficult for Don because he was Kulwicki's business manager at the time.

The Road to NASCAR

So many times Don has been called upon to minister to friends and families of NASCAR drivers who have been injured or killed. So many times he has been grateful to bring some comfort and reassurance of God's love to those who desperately need it, grateful for the ministry God has given him among the NASCAR family.

It all started when he was working for Winner Ford, and his old friend Peter Criscuolo died. Don was asked to present the eulogy, even though Don is a Protestant and Criscuolo was a Catholic. Normally, that would not be permitted in a Roman Catholic church, but because the priest knew of the special relationship between the two men, and that it had been Criscuolo's desire to have Don speak at his funeral, he made an exception. The church was clogged with people who had known Criscuolo, including senior executives from Ford Motor Company, General Motors, and the National Automobile Dealers Association.

This was a wonderful opportunity for Don to draw upon his Bible college training and present the gospel in the context of a eulogy for his friend and mentor. The experience also demonstrated to Don how the Christian ministry he once had set as his life's objective could be incorporated into his life in the car business.

He had discovered that a person doesn't need to have a church or a pulpit to be a minister. God calls believers to minister his grace and his Word wherever they are and whatever they're doing. As Don says, "The will of the Lord is not a place, it is a ministry." Don also knew that, to a large degree, the successes he had enjoyed resulted from his adherence to Christian principles in the workplace. He asked others to walk by those same principles of integrity, fair play, and hard work.

After Criscuolo's death, Don wasn't thinking very much about what he would be doing next. He was happy at Winner Ford, running a service department that had become the nationwide standard for Ford dealerships. He was finishing up all of Criscuolo's speaking engagements and conducting his own seminars at dealerships throughout the country. If one word could describe Don's life, it was content.

And that certainly meant, as it always had, that the winds of change were getting ready to blow through his life.

About this time Winner decided to enter the world of NASCAR racing by sponsoring a car in the Winston Cup series. That was how Don met Kulwicki, with whom he soon developed a close friendship. Kulwicki had won Rookie of the Year honors during his first year on the NASCAR circuit, and as his friendship with Don grew, he began talking to Don about leaving Winner Ford to join his team. Kulwicki knew he was in a good position to win the Winston Cup championship during 1992. A championship could mean enormous revenue opportunities—especially if he had the right business manager.

Don kept putting Kulwicki off because he was so comfortable at Winner Ford. And then one day he received a phone call from Joe Gibbs, former coach of the National Football League's Washington Redskins. Gibbs, a committed Christian, was putting together a racing team for the NASCAR circuit and was interested in having Don head up his team. Don was excited, not only because he and Gibbs shared the same faith, but because he had been a Redskins fan since he was a boy. And of course, there had been those wonderful days at Dorney Park and an interest in racing that went back almost as far as he could remember.

Don negotiated with the Gibbs organization for three months but could not strike a deal. That's when he started to think it was time to look in another direction.

When an offer came from Martin Birrane, who lived in London and owned the race car driven by Bobby Hillin, Don took it. Birrane interviewed Hawk over the phone, decided he was just the man he was looking for, and hired him immediately to take control of the day-to-day operations of his team. Team

Ireland, as it came to be known in NASCAR circles, competed in only fifteen races that year, and after the eleventh, NASCAR officials decided to tear down Hillin's car to check all of the engine specifications. The inspection found that one of the engine's cylinder heads was mismachined by 77 thousandths of an inch. The violation made no difference in the car's horse-power, but it wasn't in line with NASCAR specifications. The car was disqualified.

Birrane, a very proper British gentleman, felt that his honor had been tarnished by the ruling and decided to withdraw from the series rather than face further "embarrassment." He called Don and told him to sell the equipment—cars, engines, parts, everything—and fire everyone on the team. And he wanted it done right then.

Don said he couldn't do that. It wouldn't be fair to the team members, who had worked so hard and faithfully. He told Bir-rane he believed it was only fair to give them enough notice to allow them time to find jobs with other teams. Birrane thought about it and agreed that Don was right, but he still wanted the equipment sold as quickly as possible.

One prospective buyer offered top dollar for some of Team Ireland's equipment but insisted on paying cash. Don didn't want to take the money because there was no one else in the room to witness the transaction, and Birrane, some three thou-sand miles away, would never know what was offered. On the other hand, if the deal was refused, the buyer was ready to walk out the door.

After thinking about it for a couple of minutes, Don hit upon the solution. He called an associate into the room as a witness. Then he spread the buyer's one-hundred-dollar bills across the top of the copy machine and made a print, which he faxed to the team owner so he could decide whether he wanted to accept the offer. After that, Don returned the money to the prospective buyer.

The man was amazed by Don's scrupulousness and was happy when Birrane accepted his offer.

At the time, Don didn't think much about it. He just wanted to be sure that everyone involved knew he was going to handle the transaction as honestly and fairly as possible. Four years later, the man who had bought the equipment from Birrane called and asked if Don would take over as president and chief executive officer of his company and run his two race teams.

"The day I saw you spread that money out on that copy machine, I knew I was going to try to hire you one day," the man said. "I was so impressed by your honesty and the way you were looking out for the man you were working for." But that was later. With Team Ireland dissolved, it appeared, once again, that Don was going to be in need of a job.

Alan, We Hardly Knew You

As soon as the news got out that Don was available, he was approached by Larry Hedrick, owner of several car dealerships in the Charlotte, North Carolina, area. Hedrick headed up his own racing team. Soon that team included Don Hawk.

Meanwhile, Alan Kulwicki was still in the picture, occasionally calling Don and asking, "When are you going to quit stalling and come to work for me?"

"When are you going to make me a reasonable offer?" Don countered.

Kulwicki had gone on to win the 1992 Winston Cup Championship, which meant he had plenty of money to spend, but his offer was for five thousand dollars a year less than Don was making with Hedrick. Don liked Alan and wanted to work for him, but he couldn't see taking a pay cut of that magnitude, especially when he believed the team could pay a whole lot more.

Finally, Don decided to put Kulwicki's interest to the test.

"Alan, how much money do you make in an hour of signing autographs?"

Kulwicki didn't even have to stop to figure it out.

"Seven thousand, five hundred dollars."

"Okay. That means if you sign autographs for about forty-five minutes, you've made more than five thousand dollars."

"Yes, that's right."

"Well, when you get home tonight, ask yourself if it's worth forty-five minutes of signing autographs to get Don Hawk's services for a year."

Kulwicki did as Don suggested and called back the next morning to up the offer by five thousand dollars.

Another problem was Don's contract with Larry Hedrick Racing, a team that was just getting started. Don wasn't about to leave Hedrick in the lurch. He didn't operate that way. He honored his commitments, and that's what he told Kulwicki.

"I'll ask Hedrick if he will release me from my contract, but if he won't, then there's nothing I can do."

Don remembers that Larry Hedrick knew of his friendship with Kulwicki "and that I wanted to work with Alan. But at that time in NASCAR it seemed that there were wars going on every day because of people buying other people out of contracts, raiding other people's teams, and that sort of thing. But it was never like that with Larry and me. I told him how I felt, and he said, 'I don't want you to go. I want you to stay. But if that's what you've got to do, there must be a reason for it. So go do it.'"

And so in October 1992, Don Hawk took over control of Kulwicki's team, and the two began making preparations for defense of the Winston Cup championship. They made great partners. Kulwicki was as unflappable and quiet as Don was excitable and animated.

Kulwicki had a great sense of humor, but people had to get close to him to see it. And he didn't let very many get that close to him. He demonstrated that humor by the "Polish victory lap" he took at the end of every race he won—driving around the track in the opposite direction of the race while his thousands of fans roared their approval.

Kulwicki always managed to find time to pose for a picture with a fan or show some other little kindness. Given the demands on him, that wasn't always easy to do. He had only a few close friends, and that's the way he wanted it. His friends were important to him, but he wasn't the kind to pretend to be buddy-buddy with everyone.

He was one of the most intelligent men in the NASCAR ranks, and he held a degree in mechanical engineering from the University of Wisconsin at Milwaukee. His intelligence showed in his thoughtful, introspective demeanor and in his performance on the track. Like Earnhardt, he always seemed to know where to go, how to get ahead and stay ahead. Give him a loophole of any kind and he'd charge right through it. He expected his team to be run intelligently on and off the track, and he knew Don was the man to make certain it was run that way.

Something else made the Kulwicki-Hawk team unusual. Both men were Yankees—Kulwicki from Wisconsin and Hawk from Pennsylvania. NASCAR originated in the South, and even today the majority of its drivers hail from Dixie. Still, Kulwicki had a tremendous following throughout the South, and with the Winston Cup championship in hand, he saw the ranks of his fans everywhere grow rapidly.

When the 1993 season kicked off, Kulwicki's team seemed to be running to perfection. Of course, it would be a major feat to win the cup two years in a row. But it was obvious after the first few races that anyone who thought it was going to be easy to wrestle the championship away from him did not have an accurate view of the situation.

And then, the horrible telephone call came. Alan Kulwicki was gone. His twin-engine Merlin Fairchild had nosedived into the ground on final approach to the airport at Blountville, Tennessee.

The tragedy occurred on April 1, and when Don received word of the crash, he hoped someone was playing a bizarre and tasteless April Fool's Day prank. The truth quickly dawned on him that this was no joke but cruel reality, and the blow was almost more than he could take. How was it possible that Alan was dead?

As Don sat with Cyndee in the darkness of their bedroom, watching news reports of the tragedy on TV, many memories of Alan ran through his mind. He recalled how the self-effacing Kulwicki had often referred to himself as lucky and sometimes attributed his good fortune to the Saint Christopher medal he always kept close at hand, especially when he traveled. Don knew that when Kulwicki flew, that medal was often stashed under his seat.

70

This time, good-natured, quiet Alan's luck had run out. Neither engine was running when his airplane smashed into the ground. Kulwicki never had a chance.

With Kulwicki gone, Don felt a tremendous void in his life, not only because he had lost a good friend, but because his professional life also was in limbo. Where would he go from here? He felt as though the pieces of his career had been scattered all over that field with Kulwicki's aircraft.

Comforting the Brokenhearted

Don was sustained through those difficult days by his faith in Christ and his understanding that physical death is not the end. He was grateful that God had brought him into Kulwicki's life so that he could minister to his family, friends, racing team, and the entire NASCAR family during the emotionally wrenching period after Alan's death.

Less than three months after Kulwicki died, death took Davey Allison. Allison, son of racing great Bobby Allison, was only thirty-two years old.

In July Allison flew in his helicopter to Talladega Speedway to provide moral support for his good friend Neil Bonnett. Bonnett, who had suffered a serious head injury during a crash, was participating in a practice session after a long absence from racing. Allison wanted to be there for him.

It was one of those freak accidents that happen in an instant. Allison was coming in for a routine landing on the infield at Talladega. The chopper was within a foot of the ground when it suddenly shot up twenty-five to thirty feet into the air, turned to the left, then fell like a rock to the ground, scattering pieces of wreckage for seventy-five feet in all directions.

In a tragic irony, it was Bonnett who raced to the scene and pulled Allison from the wreckage. But his friend had suffered a massive head injury and never regained consciousness. He was buried next to his brother, Clifford, who had been killed in a racing accident just eleven months previously.

Despite his friend's death, Bonnett raced at Talladega, but his return was less than triumphant. Somehow his car became airborne, landed on top of another car, then punched a hole in the fence. Bonnett was not seriously injured but did receive deep bruises and a cracked rib.

On the same day, Jimmy Horton was involved in a crash that sent his car flying over the wall and down a five-story embankment. He was not injured. But in the same accident, Stanley Smith suffered a severe skull fracture and nearly bled to death after severing his carotid artery. He lost nearly half of his blood by the time paramedics got him stabilized for transport to a local hospital. He was hospitalized for forty days and was presumed dead on four occasions during that time.

As Smith was fighting for his life, Bobby Allison came to visit him five times. Smith said later, "Can you imagine how difficult it must have been for him to stand next to the room where he had watched his son die two weeks earlier?"

But as Don will attest, that's the way it is in racing. The drivers are tough, with nerves of steel. When they are out on the track, not one of them will back away from doing what it takes to win. But underneath it all, they are family, and they will do everything they can for each other when tragedy comes calling.

Reflecting on his attempt to rescue Allison from the helicopter crash, Bonnett said, "I just felt so helpless."

He also recalled some advice he had given Allison when Davey had begun talking about his desire to be a NASCAR driver. "Man, you don't need to get in this mess. I've never minded lying in the hospital with IVs hanging out of me, but I haven't ever liked to visit friends like that. If you do this long enough, it'll bite you. It's not like checkers we're playing out here."[1]

Bonnett, who was considered to be the friendliest, most likable guy in racing, lost his life in a racing accident on February 11, 1994, at the age of forty-seven. Don's skills as a minister were needed again as he sat by his friend's hospital bed and, later, as he participated in Bonnett's memorial service.

Waltrip on Hawk

Michael Waltrip, driver of Citgo car #21: I've known about Don Hawk longer than I've known him. He came around with Alan Kulwicki originally, and he's been really close to the Wood brothers, the owners of my car.

When I think of Don, I think of a guy with good Christian values—a good, solid family man. When you meet someone whose foundations are as solid as Don's, and who presents himself like he does—well, in our business, you not only remember, but you're impressed as well.

It is great for me to have a friend like Don, and I don't think it mattered what road Don chose to follow—he was going to be the type of person who gives his heart to his work, and that comes from his Christian beliefs. The Lord tells us to be our best at whatever we do, and Don's taken that very seriously.

I really like it when Don ministers at church. He says things that go straight to my heart—things I need to hear. What he says from the pulpit really sinks in and makes me challenge myself to grow in the Lord.

One other thing about Don. I think bad language is more prevalent here than anywhere else in the world, but Don doesn't ever slip. He's genuine, and that's one of the best things you can say about someone.

America's Real National Pastime

Watkins Glen, New York

It isn't a victory for Dale Earnhardt.

But then again, it is.

Two weeks after his crash at Talladega, Earnhardt has driven all 90 laps in The Bud at the Glen event and finished sixth. Relief driver David Green, who expected to pilot Earnhardt's car for much of the race, has stood on the sidelines and watched Earnhardt prove just how well Don Hawk knows him.

Although in constant pain, Earnhardt stayed in front of the pack for the first 29 laps before giving way to eventual winner Geoff Bodine, whose victory is his first in nearly two years.

From his usual vantage point in the pit, Don could only shake his head in amused amazement at his boss's heroics. Everyone else expected Earnhardt to come out of the race at the first pit stop, but Don knew better. If there was any way Earnhardt could keep driving, that was what he was going to do.

Bodine, happy to be in victory lane again after such a long absence, attributed his win to the fact that his team had "decided to make this a two-stop race—no matter what."

Bodine stuck to his strategy, and it paid off with his first win in fifty-four races as he held off a late challenge from second-place finisher Terry Labonte. Mark Martin finished third. Bodine, who started the race in thirteenth place in the thirty-nine-car field, averaged just over 92 miles per hour on the 2.454-mile road course, which features eleven turns and is considered one of the most difficult of all NASCAR tracks.

America's Fastest Growing Sport

Ask Don and he'll tell you it's heroes like Earnhardt and neck-and-neck finishes featuring drivers like Bodine and Labonte that have made NASCAR racing zoom in popularity over the past few years. What he won't tell you is that the sport's boom also is due in part to the astute business and management practices men like him have brought to the table.

And yet, after the plane crash that took Alan Kulwicki's life, Don thought seriously about leaving racing and returning to the automobile business. Don was busy for quite a while administering Kulwicki's estate, which he continues to do with Cyndee's help.

The last thing Don wanted to do at the time was attend the Bristol race, which came only days after the plane crash. He wasn't sure he could bear to be there. In fact, he didn't want to be anywhere near a racetrack.

Nevertheless, there was business to attend to, including a meeting with NASCAR President Bill France to discuss the future of the Kulwicki racing team. In fact, France wanted to meet with Don at trackside before the race. Don left the track without staying to watch the race that Rusty Wallace promised he would win in Kulwicki's name—and did.

Over the next few weeks, Don had to bury his pain and deal with the future of Kulwicki's team. Even though the team's sponsor had pulled out in a dispute over who would succeed Kulwicki, the plan was to find another driver and finish the season. The first order of business was to line up a new sponsor, and as Don would soon discover, that wasn't going to be easy.

He spent hours on the phone with prospective sponsors, finally lining up Bojangles restaurants for three races, Hanes for two more, and Matchbox Cars for another. That was only six races—well short of the thirty-one that were needed to complete the racing year—but at least it was a start.

Shortly after that, the entire team was sold to Geoff Bodine, and Don asked to be released from his contract. He had nothing at all against Bodine. It was just that the only reason Don had wanted to be a part of the team in the first place was because of his friendship with Alan. It didn't seem right for him to stay on when Alan was gone. Besides, he was finding that serving as executor of Kulwicki's estate was taking up almost all of his time. He wasn't sure he could continue to do that and do a good job for any other driver.

Meeting with the Man in Black

Don's last race as part of the Bodine-Kulwicki team was at Dover, and as fate—or somebody—would have it, Bodine's stall was next to Earnhardt's in the garage area. That's where Richard Childress, owner of Earnhardt's famous black Monte Carlo, asked Don if he would consider working for Earnhardt.

Don hadn't had much contact with Earnhardt, but he knew Childress, who had provided motors to Team Ireland.

Sport magazine has called Childress "certifiably the most deserving success story in NASCAR." On more than one occasion, NASCAR's France has called Childress "my hero" because of the way he built from "nothing" what *Sport* refers to as "the most consistently competitive team in NASCAR."[2]

Although Don knew Childress only in passing, he knew the man's reputation, and the reverse was also true.

"Of course," Don said. "Who wouldn't consider working for Dale Earnhardt?" The operative word was consider, because Don still wasn't sure he was ready to stay in the racing business.

The next day, when Earnhardt came to the track for his practice run, he sought Don out and asked if they could get together later in Earnhardt's tractor trailer for a talk. The meeting was brisk and to the point. The man in black wanted to know Don's story. He asked why Kulwicki had hired him and was interested in what Don knew about law, contracts, the car business, and racing.

Before they parted company, Earnhardt told Don he wanted him to meet his wife, Teresa. He suggested they all get together the following weekend at a race in Pennsylvania's Pocono Mountains and said he would arrange for them to fly together to the race.

Don was impressed that Earnhardt wasn't going to hire him without his wife's approval. Don valued deeply the judgment and sensibilities of his own wife, and he appreciated the fact that Earnhardt apparently felt the same way.

However, before the weekend rolled around, Don received another offer. Ricky Rudd had heard about the good work he had done with Kulwicki and wanted him to join his team.

When Don told Earnhardt about Rudd's offer, the reaction was firm. "Forget about it. You don't need to talk to anyone else."

That weekend Don talked to Teresa Earnhardt, a tall, dark-haired beauty with a dazzling smile. He found her to be intelligent, graceful, and charming. It was apparent that she took an active interest in her husband's business affairs, and equally obvious that he regarded her as a full partner. They were a team, and a very good one.

The three flew to Pennsylvania as planned, and Don answered more of their questions during the flight. That night, they had dinner together and the questions continued.

Don already had a high opinion of Earnhardt, and after spending some time in conversation with Teresa, his opinion grew. Don almost made up his mind that night to join Earnhardt's team if invited. Almost, but not quite. He wanted a few days to think about it.

Earnhardt won the Pocono race on Sunday while Don watched from the pits. As Dale and Teresa stood in victory lane acknowledging the cheers of the huge crowd, Dale motioned for Don to join them. Don shook his head and walked back into the garage area. He wasn't certain he would be joining Earnhardt's team, and he didn't think it would be right to stand up there as if he had something to do with the victory. Don also was afraid the powerful emotion of the moment might cloud his perspective and influence his decision in favor of Earnhardt's offer. As for Earnhardt, that's exactly what the driver was counting on.

When the Earnhardts returned to the garage area, they found Don waiting in their rented Chevrolet with the engine running and the door open.

Dale shot Don an amused look and asked, "How did you know to do this?"

Don shrugged. "Because I've watched you, and I've seen how quickly you get away after a race. I don't think there's anybody who gets away from a track faster than you do."

Earnhardt chuckled as he helped his wife into the car.

"Now," Don said, "I'll show you some back-road driving that'll get us to the plane in no time."

Then he did a pretty good impression of a race car driver as he shot through a confusing maze of roads all the way to the airport. Earnhardt enjoyed the ride and seemed amazed at how well Don knew the rural roads of Pennsylvania.

By the time they reached the airport, the Earnhardts had spelled out in more detail their offer to Don, and he had accepted.

It was the beginning of a great team. Earnhardt had found his man, and NASCAR's top driver had hired the business manager who was going to make the best even better.

Wood on Hawk

Eddie Wood, owner of Citgo car #21, driven by Michael Waltrip: I started to get to know Don Hawk on the telephone when he was in charge of Winner Ford's racing program. The first time we talked, it was for fifteen minutes, and we had a deal before we got off the telephone. I didn't know the man at the time, and he didn't know me.

We went along that way for several months and finally met at Daytona, when he walked right up to me and introduced himself. He was the same man back then as he is today, with more energy than ten people. Don just goes on and on and on. Never stops.

Though Don has been through some difficult times, you could tell early on that he would eventually be one of the most powerful people in the business before it was all over, and that's exactly what has happened. My brother and I have talked about it lots of times. Don Hawk knows how to get from point A to point B. He's honest. He won't tell anybody a lie. He'll deal with you one on one in a straightforward manner, and in this business—or any business—that's probably rare.

I can't explain what drives him. In my soul, I know what it is, but I can't put it into words. You've probably heard that already. It's like he's got a sixth sense about the world of NASCAR and his part in it.

He's one of the smartest guys I've ever met, and that's putting it mildly.

Don's just got a knack for being in the right place at the right time, of saying the right thing at all times, and he doesn't even have to practice it. If he goes into a meeting, or just comes around, stuff happens and it's usually good. He's a very special person who came into our world of racing at a good time.

You know, there are four of us in the company who own this race team—my dad, brother, sister, and myself. We're in the process right now of working out legally who would run things if we all went down in a plane crash. Well, that person is Don Hawk. That's how much we trust him.

This whole thing came up when we were restructuring the business and our lawyer asked what would happen if we all went down in an accident. Normally, the four of us never go up in one plane, or go anywhere together, but we thought it wise to make provision for such a possibility.

So we had our lawyers draw up something that spelled out our wishes in the event something happened to us. I gave it to

Don and he didn't even look at it. He just stuck it in his brief-case. About a week later he says, "Boy! I didn't know what you'd done!"

It was kind of funny. We trusted Don enough to put him in charge of everything, and he didn't even know it.

Back into the Whirlwind

Pocono, Pennsylvania

This day belongs to Jeff Gordon, pure and simple. And for Gordon, his victory in the UAW-Teamwork 500 is made sweeter by the fact that he lost last year's race with seven laps to go after leading most of the way. He missed a gear after a caution ended, and the few seconds it cost him to get back up to speed allowed several other drivers to pass him.

Gordon admitted that mishap was on his mind all during today's race. "I didn't know if something was going to jinx us, or if today was going to be our day."

No jinx this time. Gordon was ahead of the pack for 94 laps, averaging just under 140 miles per hour and netting nearly $97,000 for his day's work at Pocono Raceway.

Although it's been a good day for Gordon, the same can't be said for Dale Earnhardt. His black Monte Carlo stayed with the leaders for 135 laps before engine failure knocked him out of the competition. That happens from time to time, despite all attempts to prevent it. No matter what the mechanics and technicians do, there is no guarantee that an automobile engine is going to withstand the grueling pace of a 500-mile race with the accelerator pressed to the floor most of the time. Today, the engine simply couldn't do it.

Earnhardt is such a tough competitor it's just about the hardest thing in the world for him to sit and watch the other drivers out there battling for a victory. But today, that is all he could do.

A Whole Lot of Shakin' Goin' On

After Don officially joined the Earnhardt organization, there wasn't any time for sitting back and toasting the new alliance. Nor was there time for basking in the glow of Sunday's victory. There was another race the following Sunday, and plenty to do to get ready for it. For Don, it was "welcome aboard" and "get to work." For a brief moment after accepting Earnhardt's offer, Don wasn't sure he had made the right decision. He wondered how he was going to give proper attention to Earnhardt's business and continue to handle Kulwicki's estate—but he figured he'd just have to crank up the energy level another notch. It reminded him of the time he had been given the formidable task of adding a Rolls Royce dealership to a Cadillac dealership in one twenty-four-hour period. He had met that challenge, and he would meet this one, too.

Don knew right away how busy he was going to be because a typical nascar year includes more than the thirty-one races that make up the Winston Cup championship. There are also twenty nascar Craftsman Truck Series races and twenty-eight Busch Series Grand National Division races, which adds up to a total of seventy-nine races. Many of the drivers are represented in all three series, sometimes driving in both Winston Cup and Busch events, or sponsoring other teams to compete on those levels.

That means every week from February to November there's "a whole lot of shakin'" going on in the offices, garages, and meeting rooms of the NASCAR teams.

The Winston Cup circuit travels through thirteen states from New Hampshire to Florida and Delaware to California. In November 1996, NASCAR made its debut in front of a huge and enthusiastic crowd in Japan. What was once a regional sport with a rabid following primarily in the southeastern United States has grown into the most popular spectator sport in the nation, as measured by ticket sales.

It would have been one thing to join a new racing team prior to the season. It was quite another to come on board in the middle, with everything already moving ahead at full speed. Don found himself stepping back into a hurricane.

On the Monday morning following a race, the team must begin planning for the same race the following year. The day after Earnhardt's victory in the Poconos, it was time for the secretaries in what was now Don's office to start booking his Goodwrench Racing Team into hotels for the same event next year.

Decisions also were being made about transportation and personnel for the coming weekend's event. Which members of the entourage will need to be flown to the race location? Will they fly in one of three twelve-passenger King Airs, or the Learjet, or the helicopter?

By Tuesday, everyone in the organization has an itinerary detailing travel arrangements, departure and arrival times, hotel accommodations, and room assignments.

If the weekend places Earnhardt's Monte Carlo, his Busch car, and Truck Series entries on tracks three thousand miles apart, it's possible for as many as seven vehicles to begin rolling out of Charlotte, North Carolina, as early as Monday morning.

Then there's the logistical nightmare of getting everyone and everything back to Earnhardt's base in North Carolina following the race. If Earnhardt hasn't won, he escapes to a vehicle parked near an exit from the track and is whisked to the local airport, where his plane awaits.

Don is usually waiting behind the steering wheel of the get-away car, and he gets Dale to the airport as quickly as possible. But Earnhardt sits in the back seat, content to let someone else take the wheel. After spending three or more hours blasting his way around a racetrack at top speed and fighting other drivers for position, the last thing he wants to do is spend more time in freeway traffic.

Earnhardt's farm outside of Charlotte is a good location for a NASCAR driver because it is virtually in the middle of Winston Cup territory. Although NASCAR's popularity has taken it into New Hampshire, Arizona, California, and even Japan, most races are still in the southeastern United States. It takes about an hour to fly from a race in Talladega, Alabama, back to Charlotte. If traffic is good, Earnhardt can be back on his farm less than three hours after a race.

Meanwhile, the rest of his team still has miles of interstate to cover before the convoy of four souvenir tractor trailers and one souvenir supply trailer reaches home. At the same time, the Number 3 Monte Carlo is heading back in the Mr. Good-wrench trailer, which is the responsibility of the Richard Childress Racing Team. That team also is headquartered in North Carolina, about an hour north of Earnhardt's farm.

It is at least midnight of race day before all of Earnhardt's rolling stock is back in Charlotte. On Monday, Earnhardt sits down and calls Childress and the team to discuss the race. They talk about everything, including the performance of the car, the crew, and any problems that may have affected finishing position. Sometimes, after a particularly disappointing race, Earnhardt drives up to the Childress garage to give the team there a pep talk, or to provide hands-on assistance for important modifications to the car.

Also on Monday, the souvenir trailers need to be stocked for the following weekend with scores of products, all with some type of Dale Earnhardt identification: his signature, the forward-thrust number three from his Monte Carlo, or his likeness.

Forbes magazine recently estimated Earnhardt's personal income for 1997 at over $19 million a year. His income from endorsements—$15.5 million—is third highest of all active sports figures, behind only Michael Jordon and Tiger Woods. Fans buy millions of dollars worth of his merchandise every year, paying anywhere from one dollar for a bumper sticker to fifty-five hundred dollars for a custom-made leather jacket. In between those two extremes, says Don, are "the different T-shirts, earrings, belts, belt buckles, suspenders, socks, sweatshirts, jackets, hats, plaques, pictures, postcards, toy cars, clocks, watches, key chains—man, we've got it all covered. And the fans want a little bit of everything."

Don is making arrangements to add to the wide variety of Earnhardt souvenirs, including the helmets and uniforms Earnhardt has worn in races. Some Earnhardt uniforms have been sold at charity auctions for up to ten thousand dollars, a price that is not out of line with amounts paid for similar items worn by other sports superstars. Don's office holds an amazing array of souvenirs and potential souvenirs, requests for Earnhardt's services, and items from manufacturers wanting The Intimidator's endorsement. These requests for Earnhardt's time and attention seem even more amazing in light of the fact that Earnhardt dropped out of school in the eighth grade and, at age twenty-four, while married for the second time and with three children, was pumping gas for a living. He says now that his young family "probably should have been on welfare. We didn't have enough money to buy groceries."

Earnhardt may have been poor, but he had his pride and welfare was out of the question. Any thought of giving up racing also was out of the question. Earnhardt didn't have any money to spend on the sport, but he would not, *could not*, give it up.

His love for racing is something he shares with Don, and it's another element of their relationship that makes them such a great team. They understand each other's passion for racing.

The Little Sport That Grew and Grew

Since 1985, the souvenir aspect of Winston Cup racing has mushroomed into a multibillion dollar operation. In the early 1980s there may have been a total of five vendors connected with the sport. There was no television coverage and few sponsors. By the late eighties, all of that had changed. More races were being televised, and women began showing up at the tracks in increasing numbers—often with their husbands and children. Increasingly, racing was becoming a family event. It was no longer viewed as a sport reserved for "good ole boys" as people all across the country were swept up in the excitement. They were discovering that NASCAR offers thrills and excitement that most other sports can't hope to match—as the world's best and most courageous drivers do everything within their power to capture the checkered flag. All of a sudden, corporate America began to see Winston Cup racing as a gold mine waiting for the picks and shovels of marketing to begin tapping its riches.

Shav Glick, writing in the *Los Angeles Times*, observes: "The sights and sounds of big and loud American stock car look-alikes with commercials all over their sheet metal, racing door-handle-to-door-handle at 200 mph have captivated audiences like no other motor racing series, and TV is exploiting its surging popularity.

"Last year, NASCAR races had a total viewership of more than 120 million, a 25 percent increase from 1994. Already this season, TNN, the Nashville Network, and ESPN have reported record auto racing audiences. The Goodwrench 400 from Rockingham, North Carolina, brought TNN a 5.4 rating, representing 3.5 million households, and the Pontiac Excitement 400 from Richmond, Virginia, had 3.57 million viewers."

Glick quotes Bob Eaton, ESPN managing editor, as saying, "TV hasn't yet satisfied the appetite for racing of the NASCAR fan," and backs that up with the news that only professional football outdrew Winston Cup racing in head-to-head competition on television.

He also cites a *Forbes* magazine article which calls NASCAR racing "America's fastest growing professional sport." Glick writes, "That's not just motor sports, that's all sports," and adds: "Brian France, 33, NASCAR's vice president for marketing and corporate communications, is a third-generation NASCAR official who oversees a vast network of money-making adventures fueled not only by television itself, but by commercials tied to the sport. Estimated revenues for NASCAR last year were pegged at $2 billion."

He quotes France as saying, "Our drivers are our biggest asset in making fans. Fans can get right down in the garage area with the drivers, where they can talk with them. Can you imagine a baseball fan wandering out on the sidelines to chat with Barry Bonds or Cal Ripken?"[3]

Suzanne Oliver, writing in *Forbes*, backs that up: "Aware of how arrogant players have turned off sports fans, Bill France insists that NASCAR drivers treat the fans well. He puts it this way, 'We're letting the race fans into the locker room. No other sport does that.'

"Sure enough, milling around the infield at Talladega with the drivers and their crews are the guests of 25 NASCAR sponsors. When fans approach drivers for autographs and photos the drivers oblige. (Can you imagine hamming it up with a $6-million-a-year major league baseball pitcher after the game?)"[4]

NASCAR's burgeoning popularity can be seen in the fact that, as of late in 1996, seventeen of the Winston Cup tracks were busily adding seats to their grandstands. No wonder so many sponsors are clamoring to get aboard the bandwagon, including The Family Channel, Mothers Against Drunk Driving, and, because so many women are attracted to the races, Tide, Lipton Tea, Kmart, Spam, and Lowe's Home Improvement. Those sponsors are finding that NASCAR fans are particularly loyal to brands that support their favorite sport.

In her *Forbes* article, Suzanne Oliver cites statistics showing that "NASCAR fans are the most brand-loyal of all sports fans. In 1993, NASCAR sponsor Eastman Kodak polled NASCAR fans and found that 95 percent of them bought Kodak film. According to Performance Research, a marketing firm in Newport, R.I., over 70 percent of NASCAR fans consciously choose NASCAR sponsors' products over other brands."

Oliver also writes that NASCAR fans "dig deep into their pockets to view their favorite sport. NASCAR studies show that the fans travel an average of 200 miles to get to a race and, once there, spend $126 per person per race on ticket, food, lodging and souvenirs. Sales of apparel, souvenirs and collectibles licensed by NASCAR and by its drivers, have climbed from $60 million in 1990 to $400 million in 1994."[5]

In the *Los Angeles Times,* Glick writes: "Lowe's joined NASCAR last year as an experiment and, despite a poor performance by Junior Johnson's team, stepped up its sponsorship of Brett Bodine's car, even after Johnson retired and sold the team to Bodine.

"'What absolutely shocked us was the behavioral changes that took place in the consumers who were impacted by our NASCAR sponsorship,' said Dale Pond, Lowe's senior vice president. 'The first year exceeded our initial expectations.

"'Our consumers demonstrated an unbelievable affinity for Lowe's and the Team Lowe's racing concept . . . and supported it by increasing their purchases at our stores. They seem to like the fact that we are supporting NASCAR, and they seem to love the fact that they can be a part of it all.'"[6]

Still, sponsorship is only one important part of the mix that is necessary to compete successfully in Winston Cup racing. The total racing package is a mammoth undertaking, and that's understating the case. Anyone who thinks about entering the world of NASCAR needs cars to race, parts, tools, lifts, garage facilities where cars can be built and modified, transport vehicles to move men and equipment around the country, and about a thousand other items that fall under the heading of "equipment." All of these things are necessary before any sponsor climbs on board.

Once sponsorship is secured, the owner of the racing team must be certain there are enough dollars to hire the right driver and a quality pit crew. After all, no sponsor wants to pour millions of dollars into a racing effort that falls flat. Every sponsor wants to back a winner.

After sitting across boardroom tables with sponsors and negotiating a number of contracts, Don Hawk can tell you that every sponsor in NASCAR racing wants the exposure winning will provide.

The way to start building a winning team is to build a good race car. To do that requires attracting quality people to the team. And to attract quality people, a team must have a good reputation.

Don will tell you that Earnhardt scores well on all three counts. Each of his race teams is designed to be of championship caliber. He uses new equipment in all his cars. Each car is rebuilt or refurbished every week. His Winston Cup shop has eleven race cars—twelve or thirteen counting the new ones being assembled to take the place of the next two that will rotate out of circulation.

Don believes that to build a champion today in Winston Cup racing takes between seven and twelve million dollars. Without that kind of money to put into it, a team is not likely to build a consistent winner.

The cost of the tractor-trailer that transports the two race cars to tracks around the country is somewhere between $200,000 and $300,000. The cars ring in at $100,000 apiece. Below the cars in separate trailer compartments are four racing engines, which cost between $35,000 and $45,000 apiece, depending on who built them. The trailer also holds extra new transmissions, axles, brakes, rotors, calipers, and hubs. And in case the car should hit the wall, there is always an extra nose and tail in the trailer for a quick fix.

In addition to the tremendous costs of hardware, there is the expense of moving it to the various racetracks week after week. To do that as efficiently and cost-effectively as possible, everyone on the team must know his or her job and perform it flawlessly. People have to work together like members of a symphony orchestra who are playing a complicated piece of music.

A three- to four-page checklist is taped to the side of the car every Sunday morning before a race. Everyone on the team is personally responsible for one to twelve items on the checklist and must initial the line item when each job is completed: check and repack wheel bearings, check shifter operation, check clutch pedal, check gas pedal, check for Dale's goggles, check for Dale's helmet . . . and on it goes.

He Saw the Potential

It was Earnhardt, back in 1985, who first put a souvenir van on the track in Martinsville, Virginia. Today, seventy-six vendors are set up to do business for NASCAR drivers. Hundreds of offers for public appearances come in every week for someone like Earnhardt, who is considered by many to be the Michael Jordan of NASCAR. It is up to Don to handle those requests, to sort out the should-do's and the good ideas from the requests that are impossible to meet or that wouldn't be a good idea.

These days, it seems that just about everybody wants Dale Earnhardt, and even though Don has to turn down roughly 90 percent of the requests, one of his jobs is to reject them as politely and graciously as possible. Some of the requests come from small organizations wanting to bring Earnhardt in as a dinner speaker, and there is simply no way he can honor all of them, even for worthwhile charitable causes. There is only so much he can do. Don not only has a knack for cutting through all of the confusion and sorting out what moves are best for Earnhardt's business, he also has the ability to turn people down with grace and aplomb in a way that doesn't leave them angry with Earnhardt or NASCAR.

Looking for Phonies

Another of Don's jobs is spotting black market items, phony trading cards, and merchandisers who are seeking to make a dollar off Earnhardt without getting his endorsement or his permission.

Don told a reporter from *Sports Illustrated*, "The black market in NASCAR has got to be worth several million dollars a quarter—in pictures, plaques, die-cast cars, collectibles."[7]

As the reporter sat in his office, Earnhardt was busily signing hundreds of autographs for fans. Suddenly, he stopped signing and flipped a card in Hawk's direction. "Hey, Don!"

Don took one look and knew it was a phony. "That's a bootleg card," he said, advising Earnhardt not to sign it.

"If you endorse it, you're saying it's legal," he said.

Someone had gotten Earnhardt to sign a bootleg card at a racetrack, put it on a laser machine, made a copy, and turned it into a trading card, without a contract or an agreement of any kind.

"Fans send the stuff in to get it signed," Earnhardt says, "and I can't sign it, and they get mad."

He sighs and turns back to the huge stack of other cards awaiting his signature.

Labor of Love

Don obviously enjoys what he's doing and gets extremely excited when asked to compare his man against some of the biggest names in sports merchandising—Michael Jordan of the Chicago Bulls, Shaquille O'Neal of the Los Angeles Lakers, Emmitt Smith and Troy Aikman of the Dallas Cowboys. Don believes that Earnhardt's visibility and popularity are increasing at such a rate that he'll soon be right up there with any of those sports figures, and perhaps even be able to beat them out in competition for marketing dollars.

If Earnhardt had the time or the inclination, Don could book speaking engagements for him at the rate of two per day, at twenty-five thousand dollars per appearance, and keep him busy for the next two years. When Earnhardt appeared on the QVC shopping network, he sold one million dollars worth of merchandise within two hours. When he left the studio, more than one thousand callers were still holding, waiting to make their purchases. On ESPN's *Shoptalk* program, a one-hour segment netted sales of seven hundred thousand dollars.

No wonder Don is so high on Earnhardt's marketing potential.

Allegiance to their hero sets Earnhardt's fans apart. Some people seem to switch to a new favorite driver every year, but Earnhardt's fans are loyal from race to race and year to year, no matter how their man is doing in the point standings.

At NASCAR events, it seems that nearly everybody wants a souvenir to take home—a small reminder of a favorite car, driver,

93

or racing team. The same people come back repeatedly to buy more souvenirs. On any given Sunday, people stand in line for two hours or more to get to the counter of one of Earnhardt's souvenir vans. Even a quick survey of the souvenir vans will show that, whatever his standing in the battle for the Winston Cup championship, Earnhardt has already won the souvenir rush. Almost every weekend it is the same—the crowds around his trailers are two to three times the size of those around the trailers set up for his competitors, partly due to the astute marketing of Don Hawk.

A major contributor to the sales success is Sports Image, Earnhardt's marketing company. Hawk had negotiated in 1995 with his boss to purchase Sports Image, and the company, with its catalog of merchandise, has helped to push sales of Earnhardt memorabilia to around forty million dollars a year.

In 1989, fans could choose from four Earnhardt hat styles. Now there are eighteen. The same is true of T-shirts. Sports Image has a vision of Dale Earnhardt that will satisfy almost every fan, whether that vision is of Earnhardt as seven-time Winston Cup champion, man on a mission, The Intimidator, or what have you.

Selecting merchandise to be marketed each year is one of the more important of Don's jobs, and he does it in close cooperation with Dale and Teresa. Products are strewn all over the floor, chairs, couches, and tables in Dale's huge office, waiting for the process that determines which will be marketed. Most products are rejected for any number of reasons, including unfavorable price, poor quality, or unsuitable image for Earnhardt. The winners join hundreds of other catalog selections.

Like the slanted number on Earnhardt's Monte Carlo, the team's merchandising effort pushes forward. If a product doesn't drive sales, it is removed from the mix and replaced with one that does. Even products that have done well in the marketplace are rotated out of circulation after a time. The infrastructure set up by Teresa Earnhardt is still in place:

1. Don't sell Dale everywhere.
2. Strive to keep the demand greater than the supply.

3. Always have the ability to say no.

4. Say no often.

The team knows that keeping fans reaching for more souvenirs makes better business sense than drowning them in a surplus that could dilute the effect of what Don refers to as "the Earnhardt mystique."

The power of Earnhardt's name was evident in the purchase of Earnhardt's Lear jet. The airplane cost in the neighborhood of four million dollars, but Don negotiated a one million dollar reduction in exchange for the use of Earnhardt's name and image in Lear jet advertising.

Another example of Earnhardt's strength in the marketplace came at the end of Don's contract negotiations with a major trading card company. The company had been trying to include Earnhardt in its racing cards for several years. When the deal was finally arranged, Don was in California to sign the seven-figure contract and pick up a substantial check. Before he left, he managed to sweeten the arrangements for the Earnhardt organization by mentioning that Dale owns *Racing for Kids* magazine.

Because children are a big market for trading cards, Don thought the card company might want to place some ads in the magazine. The company saw Don's logic immediately, and added fifty thousand dollars to the original arrangement.

The fact that Don Hawk and Dale Earnhardt make a powerful business team is not lost on others who are closely associated with NASCAR. Some are good-naturedly envious of their business success. Wayne Estes, media relations representative for Ford Motor Sports recently said, "You know, it breaks my heart every time I see what a good team Hawk and Earnhardt make. I used to say, 'Man, the last thing Ford Motor Company or any of us in racing needs is for Dale Earnhardt to have that part of his business straightened out. If Hawk goes in there, that's going to be the last element that Earnhardt needs to be just megasuccessful.'"

Sam Bass, owner of Sam Bass Illustration and Design, and a man who is known for his captivating paintings of NASCAR

95

action, says, "Everybody out there knows that Dale's one of a kind, a unique talent, and Don's representation has made Dale's appeal and his presence in the sport even more established and powerful. That's really saying something."

Race-car owner Felix Sabates, who was closely associated with Don during his time with Alan Kulwicki, enjoys telling of the day he received a telephone call from Earnhardt, who said of Don, "Man, this guy's great!"

"I told you he was," Sabates replied.

"So, what do you think he can do?"

"Dale," Sabates said, "he can do everything. I mean, he can shine the car, run your business operation, and control your money."

Sabates on Hawk

Felix Sabates, owner of car #42, driven by Kyle Petty: I met Don before he got involved with racing. I always thought he was one of the nicest guys in the world and believed he should have been a preacher. He was always talking about the Lord. Then he moved down South and started hanging around with us at the racetrack.

Alan Kulwicki and I were very close friends, and Don knew Alan from the time Don was working at Winner Ford. When Alan told me he was going to hire Don, I thought it was a great move because he needed a business manager and Don had a lot of savvy and business experience. Plus, I think Don is one of those people with the utmost amount of integrity.

When Alan died, Don and I pretty much handled the estate, and that's when I really got to know the man. I realized the kind of loyalty and dedication he has for the person he works for. Even though Alan was gone, when Don spoke of him it was like he was still here: "Alan would want to do it this way," or "Alan would be happy if we did it this way."

It was a difficult situation because I had lost a very good friend and Don had lost both a friend and a boss. We worked very well together trying to get everything done the proper way so no one would get hurt.

I think Don is pretty much a perfectionist. He wants to be and do better than expected because he doesn't want to disappoint anybody.

Don brings a sense of unity to NASCAR because he tries to work with everybody. See, a lot of business managers just want to take care of their guy. But Don is always trying to help other people. He helped me with a deal the other day that came to more than a quarter million dollars that I was in jeopardy of losing. I called Don and explained to him and Earnhardt what was going on, because they had dealings with the same outfit that was giving me a problem. Don picked up a phone, called the guy, and said his dealings with Earnhardt would be over if he didn't settle up with me. The next day, I got a check.

He does a lot of things because he's trying to make sure everybody gets a fair shake.

A Typical Day at the Racetrack

Concord, North Carolina

This week should have been good for Don Hawk, Dale Earnhardt, and the rest of the Goodwrench Racing Team. After all, Charlotte Motor Speedway, site of the Coca Cola 600, can be considered the home track for the team, which is headquartered nearby.

If there is such a thing as a home track advantage, though, Earnhardt's team wouldn't be the only one to benefit from it. Nearly a third of NASCAR's most successful drivers make their homes in and around Charlotte, so this is "old home week" for a lot of the teams.

Besides, things don't always work out the way you want them to, and this week hasn't been much fun from the start.

It all began when practice was held up after NASCAR inspectors ruled several cars had inferior tubing in the roll cages. Sixteen drivers, including Earnhardt, were held out of practice for the same problem. The delay was annoying, time-consuming, and expensive for everyone—but NASCAR expects its rules and standards to be followed precisely. Although the drivers may not like it, they understand that has to be the case, for the sake of fair play and their safety.

Still, it hurts to lose valuable practice time.

And for the Goodwrench folks, that hurt was magnified today, when Dale Jarrett dominated the race, leading for the final 62 laps and finishing 11.98 seconds—more than one-third of a lap—ahead of Earnhardt. It was Jarrett's day from start to finish, and every time Earnhardt or another driver began to make a move, he found an extra boost of energy. He also had the benefit of a trouble-free race. His car was perfection from green flag to winner's circle.

Earnhardt is pleased by his second-place finish—and with good reason. He started in forty-third position and moved up to challenge for the lead. Midway through the race, it looked like his car was spent, along with his energy. He began to falter badly, drifting toward the back of the pack. But over the last fifty or so laps, he began moving up again. He had the capacity crowd on its feet, cheering and yelling during the last ten laps. He couldn't catch Jarrett, but he made a race out of it, and that was reason enough to be proud. Earnhardt has no doubt that if the race had gone another fifty laps the outcome would have been different.

As Jarrett stood in victory lane acknowledging the huge crowd's ovation, he said, "We're going to see if we can win us a million bucks come Labor Day. If you're going to win just a few, it's good to win the big ones."

Jarrett was referring to the one-million-dollar bonus Winston Cup sponsor R. J. Reynolds Tobacco Company offers each year to any driver who wins three of the four races considered to be NASCAR's jewels. They are the Coca Cola 600, the Daytona 500, because it has the richest purse of all NASCAR races, the Mountain Dew Southern 500 at Darlington, South Carolina, because it is run on NASCAR's oldest super speedway, and the Winston Select 500 at Talladega, Alabama, which is considered to be the fastest track. Bill Elliott, the only driver ever to claim the one-million-dollar prize, averaged 212 miles per hour at Talladega the year he did it and earned the nickname Million-Dollar Bill in the process.

100

Jarrett laughingly told reporters that Million-Dollar Dale might not have the same ring to it, but he would be happy to settle for that. Because he won the season-opening Daytona 500 and finished second in the Winston Select 500, he could win the bonus on September 1 in Darlington.

Here in Charlotte, Jarrett averaged 147.578 miles per hour, and won $165,250 for his first-place finish.

The Will to Win

By the end of today's race, Don was exhausted, and it showed. Anyone taking a close look at him probably would think he had been out on the track for all six hundred miles himself. And in a way, he had been. He had spent nearly every ounce of his considerable energy trying to will Dale Earnhardt an extra boost of speed and energy that would help him catch the leader.

What energy didn't go toward Earnhardt's black Number 3 had been spent encouraging and exhorting his pit crew in their work and doing whatever possible to lend a hand. Although Don is Earnhardt's business manager, he doesn't let his job stop there. On race day, he's one of the team. As in the time he splattered white paint all over his suit, Don has never been afraid of a little dirt, oil, or grease.

Today Don was on his way to the track well before 6 A.M. And even though the starting flag wouldn't drop for several hours, already bumper-to-bumper traffic stretched for several miles approaching the speedway. Don noted license plates from all over the country—from Maine to Florida, Michigan to Texas, and New Hampshire to California. He was reminded that what Suzanne Oliver wrote in *Forbes* is true: "The traffic leans heavily toward Chevrolet Monte Carlos, Thunderbirds and Dodge pickups; this isn't your Volvo/BMW/Lexus crowd."

Earnhardt's crew had been on the scene for several hours. Danny "Chocolate" Myers, who is Earnhardt's "gasman," always arrives at the track well before sunup on race day, and today was no exception. Chocolate's job is to set up the pits, which means he has to unload the pit cart, make sure there are three

101

full cans of fuel, and get everything else into position to ensure the maximum speed and efficiency of each pit stop.

Fans were pouring into the grandstands, and some headed straight for the pits. Although the teams have a lot of work to do at such times, they find time to talk to fans, smile for photos, and sign autographs.

But once the green flag drops, every member of the crew must be alert and ready to respond at all times. Most of the time, there is nothing to do for the first fifty laps or so. But something can go wrong at any time, and if it does, the crew can't lose a moment because of inattention or unpreparedness.

Everyone in the pit wears a radio and headset. Most crew members are listening to Earnhardt's frequency, but others are tuned to NASCAR, the competition, or Motor Racing Network. Chocolate Myers listens to two frequencies at once, trying to pick up any extra tidbits of information that will give Earnhardt the slightest advantage.

Earnhardt's spotters let him know if they see any trouble spots on the track: "Spin behind you, Dale. Trouble behind you. Debris down low—stay high."

Meanwhile, everyone else in the pit area tries to anticipate what will have to be done during the first stop. Will the car need two new tires or four? Will the chassis need an adjustment? Everyone knows that the simplest change can make the difference between a visit to victory lane and a finish far out of the money.

As time for the first pit stop approaches, all the crew members are in position and ready to spring into action. Suddenly the crew chief yells that there will be a pit stop on Earnhardt's next trip around the track. When the big Monte Carlo comes rolling in, seven crew members leap over the pit wall and take care of the driver's needs. Myers' job is to stick the nozzle of the ninety-pound gas can into the tank and get as much fuel as possible into the car before Earnhardt jams it into gear, floors the accelerator, and screams back onto the track.

One crew member operates the jack. Another loosens the lugnuts. All around the car, the crew moves in a precise choreography that comes from years of working together. They must anticipate the others' moves down to the split second. When Myers needs his second can of gasoline, another crewman has to be ready to hand it to him. There can be no slips, nobody in the wrong place for even an instant.

Today, the pit crew was in perfect sync, and the first stop went off without a hitch. Earnhardt was ready to get back in the race within twenty seconds. For a few seconds, after he floored it and headed back onto the track, Myers ran along behind, intent on getting every possible drop of gasoline into the car. The last thing he wants is for additional pit stops to become necessary because the car is low on fuel.

As soon as the black Monte Carlo was back on the track, Myers weighed his cans of 108 octane gasoline and quickly calculated how much fuel he was able to get into the big car's tank. That let him know when the next fuel stop would be required.

In the pits, nothing is left to chance or taken for granted.

Don Hawk was so full of energy today it wouldn't have been surprising to see him out there with the pit crew, changing tires and checking the oil. But NASCAR's rules are specific and firm. No more than seven people over the pit wall at a time. And when they're out there working on the Monte Carlo, the only thing the rest of the team can do is cheer them on.

Practice Makes Close to Perfect

Don believes that Richard Childress builds one of the toughest, most durable, most competitive cars on the NASCAR circuit. He has one of the best teams out there, and part of what makes them that good is that they have been together for so long. It takes many employees to build and maintain such an effective racing team. In Earnhardt's shop alone, at least two dozen people work on the car, from building the engine to fabricating the body. And there are more than forty other racing teams on the circuit.

During a typical race week, Monday is given over to fixing or rebuilding whatever broke down or was damaged during Sunday's race. Tuesday, the reconditioning process continues, and on Wednesday, the car is put together so the tractor-trailer can be on its way to the next location that night.

The same car isn't used in all races because the NASCAR circuit includes road courses, super speedways, and short tracks. Each demands a different type of car with an alternate race setup. A flat track calls for one type of car, a highly banked track another. A highly banked track that's two-and-a-half miles long calls for yet another car. Having the right vehicle for each track is essential.

For example, a road course car has to be able to turn right and left. On an oval track, the cars just keep turning left. Consequently, for a road race, the car is sprung so that when it's put into a right turn, the shock absorbers on that side of the car rebound and lift the rear and side of the car up to a level position. The car then is ready for the left turn that's coming. The roll center and center of gravity on the car must be set to permit the car to balance itself when it moves through the middle of a highly banked corner or the center of a flat track or a road course corner. Balance is crucial. The car has to quickly return to a level balance, but it takes engineers to figure out the mechanics. That's why Earnhardt has engineers on his payroll as well as shock specialists and engine specialists—people who do only one thing and do it exceptionally well. NASCAR racing is a far more sophisticated sport than it used to be, and it gets more technical every year. To compete successfully, a team needs specialists.

Don likes to quote the famous evangelist Dwight L. Moody, who said, "I'd rather have said of me, 'This one thing he did,' than 'These forty things he dabbled in.'"

Testing: Another Key to Success

Testing the car also is important, and NASCAR allows each team seven test dates for each car. So, there's a solid advantage to having more than one car, because that allows more time for testing, fine-tuning, and improving on what the team knows.

If Don had his way, he'd reduce the number of test dates, because he knows some teams on the circuit simply don't have the money to build a second or third car. He believes that giving extra test dates to teams with multiple cars gives them an unfair advantage.

As far as the Childress team is concerned, Earnhardt is dead-set against the idea of having a teammate. When Childress has brought up the subject, Earnhardt has replied, "Richard, let me tell you something. I'm going to view him as one more car I have to beat. So don't tell me he's my teammate."

Thumbs Up for a Job Well Done

In the pits during today's race, the members of Earnhardt's crew scrambled back over the wall to get ready for the next stop. Don tried to get Myers' attention and gave him a thumbs-up for a job well done, but Chocolate was moving so fast he didn't seem to see it.

Myers and Hawk do see eye to eye on a lot of things related to racing, including the fact that no one should allow the sport to come first in life. With Chocolate Myers and Don Hawk, it is God first, family second, and then racing.

Myers doesn't look like anyone's idea of a preacher. Standing six feet, five inches tall, weighing two hundred sixty-five pounds, and sporting a dark beard and a spider tattoo on one arm, he seems more like the type of guy who can't wait for the race to be over so he can go out and raise Cain. There was a time when that might have been an accurate description, but no longer.

"Since I put my priorities in order, life's really changed dramatically for me, and it's changed for the good," Myers told *Sports Spectrum* magazine's Brett Honeycutt. "The hardest thing I ever did was walk through the church doors, and the easiest thing I ever did was stay in the church doors.

"Being a Christian is a fun thing. . . . I still have a good time. I have fun. I still pick and play (with people), but I've cleaned up my act. It's the greatest thing that ever happened to me.

"If everybody had a clue how much God could change their life, everybody would do it," he said. "I think people think, 'Being a Christian, that's going to be some boring, humdrum life.' But that's as far from the truth as it's going to get."[8]

Humdrum is one thing life is not, for either Myers or Hawk, although Don has to admit he wishes at times his life would slow down, at least a little bit.

Myers on Hawk

Danny "Chocolate" Myers, crew member, Childress Racing Team: When I think of Don Hawk, I remember the first time he came around several years ago. He was a different kind of guy, with very strong Christian beliefs, and I just didn't think he fit in with the racing crowd. Just shows you how wrong you can be.

I found out that he was a hustler—in the best sense of the word—when he was with Alan Kulwicki and those guys. It seemed that he always had a deal cooking. And as the sport has grown over the past few years, I think that instead of Don catching up with NASCAR racing, the sport has caught up with him.

I also think Don Hawk and Dale Earnhardt make a good team. Dale is a very busy man with a lot of people watching his time. If the truth be known, he could probably be signing autographs twenty-four hours a day, seven days a week. Of course he doesn't have time to do that, so it's good that he's got Don to assist him, telling him what he should and shouldn't do, helping him make the most of his time.

Don's really a very nice guy, and he's sharp, always wide awake and at it. He's always doing something, taking care of Dale. He's done a lot for Dale Earnhardt and for the Childress Racing Team.

Life on the Road

Loudon, New Hampshire

It is a hot, humid day in New England, but as far as Ernie Irvan is concerned, it is the most beautiful day he has seen in a long, long time.

In front of eighty thousand screaming fans, he has won his first race in more than two years, completing a remarkable battle back from near death.

Irvan, who was critically injured in a crash at Brooklyn, Michigan, on August 20, 1994, said, "Until you win, you never know if you're going to do it again." Acknowledging that some people said he would never be able to regain his form and had been urging him to retire from racing, he said, "Maybe this will shut them up."

Irvan had been hospitalized for several weeks following his near-fatal crash, and was unable to race at all for fourteen months.

At New Hampshire International Speedway today, he started in 6th position, stayed among the leaders throughout, and took

107

control of the race after Jeff Gordon lost power on the 237th lap. Gordon, who was 3rd in the Winston Cup point standings going into the race, was slowed by two ignition failures and wound up 34th.

Earnhardt did not fare much better. He finished back in the pack and saw Terry Labonte, who finished 6th, move past him and into 1st place in the point standings.

Still, Earnhardt seemed happy to see Irvan make it all the way back into the winner's circle, and said, "Hats off to Ernie. His team stuck behind him and he made it back to victory lane. He did a great job, and it's great to see him back in the winner's circle."

The Downside of Life in the Spotlight

From Atlanta to Loudon, from Charlotte to Brooklyn, the main problem for Don is that he has to be away from his family so much of the time. If he could do his job at home, he would, but that's impossible. His life is a succession of airplanes, helicopters, and expressways. Days go by when he has to be content with making phone calls to home, and nothing more.

Cyndee Hawk says she gets tired of hearing people say how much they envy the life she and Don have. People see the excitement, the glamour, the time spent in the spotlight, but they don't see the downside of it all. Cyndee would like to have her husband home more often, but much of the time she's left to cope with household emergencies or attend her children's functions by herself.

She would love to be able to sit on the couch with her husband, watching television in the evenings and perhaps falling asleep with her head in his lap, or sit quietly with him and discuss events of the day after the kids are in bed. Such moments happen occasionally for Don and Cyndee, but not often enough to suit either of them. And Don is always disappointed when he has to miss one of the kids' baseball games, a piano recital, or a school play. He's had to swallow hard more than once when one of his children has asked him if he will be able to attend a "big event," and he has to say he's sorry but he's going to be out of town . . . again.

Don's traveling also makes his family worry. Only a series of unforeseen circumstances kept him from being on Alan Kulwicki's plane the night it crashed into a Tennessee field. Don remembers how he and Cyndee cried together as they watched the late-night news reports of that tragedy. Their children, Jessica, Julie, Jennifer, and John, were awakened by the noise and came as a group to their parents' bedroom to see what was happening. When the children saw their parents' tears, some of them, too, began to cry.

The children knew and liked Alan Kulwicki, and Don believes that as they stood there in tears, absorbing the horrible event that had just occurred, a fear began to grow in the back of their minds. They knew that their daddy could have been on that airplane, and if he had been, he never would have come home.

Since that day, it has been harder for all of them to kiss Don good-bye when he has to head out on the road.

"Do you have to go again, Dad?"

"Do you have to fly this time?"

"When are you going to be home?"

Those are the questions that let him know the Kulwicki tragedy is still playing in the back of their minds. Don hates it that his children carry that burden around with them, but there's nothing he can do about it except remind them that his life is in God's hands and that God is to be trusted in all things. Besides, even if anything should happen to him, they have the assurance of knowing that they will be together again in eternity because they have all surrendered their lives to Christ. The girls are old enough to begin to understand and accept that frequent traveling is a part of their father's life, and their anxious questions are being replaced by little reminders—such as notes slipped into his overnight bag—that they love him, miss him, and will be praying for him when he is gone. But son John still struggles with his anxieties.

When Don went to Japan to promote NASCAR racing, John had dozens of questions about the trip.

"What are you going to do if the plane has trouble while it's flying over the ocean? How far are you going to be from a place you can land? How many hours does it take to cross the ocean?" He kept asking questions until the moment of his father's departure.

Big Weekend in Richmond

John, the youngest of the Hawk children and the only boy, is particularly close to his dad and seems to have inherited his interest in racing. For that reason, every year on his birthday, John travels with his father to Richmond, Virginia, for the Miller 400. It makes him feel grownup and important to spend a few days with his father—just two guys baching it for a while.

Race weekend is hectic, and there are precious few hours that are not spent either at the track or in race preparation. But finally, at the end of a long day, father and son are alone in their hotel room, able to kick off their shoes and relax. Like kids everywhere, John loves being in a hotel and enjoys the feeling of being on vacation it gives him. It makes school seem so far away. Most of all, he loves being alone with his dad.

"Dad, you want to watch some TV?"

"Sure." Don hands his son the remote control.

"What do you want to watch?" John begins flipping through the fifty-plus channels offered by the hotel's cable system.

"I don't know. Why don't you decide?"

"Me?" It may be a small thing, but John's eyes open wide with excitement. As the youngest in a family with three sisters and two parents, it's not often that John gets to control the remote, much less decide by himself what to watch. He eventually settles on a basketball game on ESPN, which Dad thinks is a wonderful choice. Although it doesn't rate up there with racing, basketball has always been one of Don's loves. He follows the NBA and enjoys spending some time in the yard shooting hoops with the kids, all of whom, he says, are dead-eye shooters.

As the game continues, Don grabs the room-service menu.

"Getting hungry? You want something to eat?"

110

"But, Dad," John protests, "I didn't see a restaurant."

"Well, you know what, John? We're going to stay right here and have them bring our dinner to our room."

"Really? We can really do that?"

"You bet we can."

"Cool."

Everything about this experience is super cool to John. For a brief weekend it doesn't matter that his dad is gone so often while he stays home with his mom and three sisters. This weekend, John is with his father at a NASCAR Winston Cup race in Richmond, Virginia, ordering room service, exercising total power over the remote control, and watching basketball games on television until well past his normal bedtime. There's not much in the world that could be better than this.

Except, perhaps, race day.

At the race, John's royal treatment continues. Members of the Richard Childress team treat him like he's their own son, probably because so many of the crew are away from their families this weekend. There's good-natured joshing and kidding, all in a spirit of fun, and it makes John smile like the Cheshire Cat to be the center of so much attention.

"Hey, Don, I see you brought your partner with you."

"You'd better look out. He'll have your job in no time."

And of course, "Hey, Don, you've got a very handsome son, here. He must take after his mother."

Chocolate Myers fashions a makeshift seat for John on top of the toolbox in the Goodwrench pit area to give him a better view of everything that's going on, and then places him on his perch. John seems a little unsure at first, but after a quick look around, his face breaks into a broad grin. He loves it up there.

"Here, man, you can't be part of the crew without this." Chocolate reaches over and places a headset around the boy's neck. "Let me see, what else do you need?"

He looks around and sees one of the crew members drinking a can of Sun Drop Soda.

"Oh, yeah." Myers pops open a can and hands it to John. "We drink an awful lot of this stuff during the race. It gets hot in here."

111

He looks John over from head to toe.

"Now," he finally says, "you look official."

Sure enough, John looks like an official member of the crew, and with his very own headset, he's ready for an exciting afternoon, watching the action and listening to anything Earnhardt and his crew talk about during the race. John's getting an insider's view of NASCAR racing that most people will never have, and it's an experience neither he nor his father will forget.

Don obviously enjoys having his son with him. He can go on for hours about each of his children and how they have contributed to his success as a businessman and a person. Tears come into his eyes when he talks about an incident that occurred a few months ago as he unpacked his bags at the start of another four-day stay away from home.

As he unzipped his garment bag, he felt something lumpy down in one of the pockets. He didn't remember putting anything there, so he reached in to see what it was and pulled out John's favorite teddy bear—Cubby Bear. John hadn't wanted his dad to be alone and had sent him some company for the long trip. Don slept with the little bear, with its short crewcut hair and muscular body, because it made him think of his son, and the rest of his family, and how happy he was that they would be there to welcome him home in a few days.

He cried, too, because his little boy's act of love reminded Don of the costs involved with the life he leads.

Howard on Hawk

Richard F. Howard, president and CEO, WSMP Inc., sponsor of cars driven by Dale Earnhardt and Jeff Green: Don's a good guy and he's become a great friend. The friendship is important to me all by itself, but in addition, when a sponsor is spending the kind of dollars necessary to even be in racing, it's important to know somebody on a pretty good basis. Sometimes you have to be pretty aggressive with each other. It helps when the man you're negotiating with is a good guy and a friend.

Another thing about Don: I think he's one of those people you'll find in the world of sports who will themselves to win. I mean, he's not the one who's out there racing or playing ball, but at the same time, he wants to be the best he can be. When the real tough times come along, his will comes into play, and he eventually works out the solution.

Everywhere Don has been in racing, the people speak highly of him—the Bonnett family, the Wood family, the Kulwicki family . . . everyone.

On the Road Again

Indianapolis, Indiana

Don Hawk woke up today not quite sure where he was. Charlotte? Atlanta? Oh yes . . . the fog lifted and he remembered. Indianapolis, Indiana, home of the world famous Indianapolis 500 and—today—the 160-lap Brickyard 400.

It's easy to forget where you are sometimes, at least for a moment, when you spend so much time on the road and when you are missing your wife and family.

Everywhere Don goes, he has more than racing on his mind. There are meetings with potential new sponsors and people who want to grab a ride on the fast-moving coattails of NASCAR's booming popularity. But first things come first, and before Don checks over today's schedule, he pulls a worn piece of paper from his overnight bag. That piece of paper is one of the best gifts Cyndee ever gave him, and he's pulled it out and looked at it a thousand times—or more.

115

On the Hawks' wedding anniversary a few years ago, at the suggestion of one of their daughters, Cyndee sat down and wrote out "100 Reasons Why I Love You" for her husband. Don is not an overly sentimental or emotional man, but he admits to fighting back a few tears the first time he read Cyndee's list of reasons for her devotion to him. Since that day he's carried it with him everywhere. Along with his unshakable faith in God, it is one of Don's most important sources of strength for the battle.

Don will readily admit that some of Cyndee's reasons for loving him may sound bizarre. Some are silly. But others are serious and personal. One of these days, Don thinks, he is going to sit down and write out two hundred reasons why he loves his wife. Someday . . . soon . . . when he has time. But when that will be is hard to tell.

Earnhardt tries to give Don time to spend with his family.

"Don," he will say, "you don't have to come on this trip. Why don't you sit this one out and spend the weekend with your wife and kids?"

But Don invariably has some important meetings set up, so there's no way he can stay home. This August day in Indianapolis is no exception.

By the time Don finishes with the first of his meetings and arrives at Indianapolis Motor Speedway, the stands are beginning to fill. Before the green flag drops they will be filled to capacity with more than three hundred thousand screaming race fans who will be treated to a dandy of a battle. Unfortunately, Dale Earnhardt doesn't figure in what will turn out to be a two-car battle for the checkered flag. This day will belong to the Fords, specifically, the Fords belonging to Ernie Irvan and Dale Jarrett.

The lead changes hands several times before Jarrett takes the lead for good just seven laps from the finish. Jarrett passes Irvan when his teammate goes a little too high into a turn and has trouble keeping his car under control. By the time Irvan can regain full speed, Jarrett has built a comfortable lead. He finishes more than six car lengths in front while his crew crowds

116

along the pit wall, waving and shouting encouragement as their man drives under the checkered flag.

"I always watched the races here at Indianapolis, and it's a tremendous feeling to be in this victory lane," Jarrett says. He has won more than five hundred thousand dollars from a total purse of nearly five million dollars. But for Jarrett, the best part of the day is that it has provided a great tuneup for Labor Day and the million-dollar payday he hopes is awaiting him in Darlington, South Carolina.

Meanwhile, Back at the Ranch

As soon as the race is over, Don reaches for the portable phone he always carries to call home and find out how things are going. That's something he does every day while he's on the road. He wants Cyndee and the kids to know he's thinking about them, and he also wants to feel that he's a part of their lives, even though he may be several hundred miles away.

When he talks to Cyndee, he's always amazed at the grace and good humor with which she handles the many emergencies that come along, and today is no exception. Although at times she's exhausted and aggravated, she never says, "Don, you've got to quit all this traveling and find another job."

Cyndee grew up in a racing family, but it was horse racing that took her father away from home for days at a time. That lifestyle wasn't something she wanted for herself. When she and Don were married, she thought he would still wind up in the ministry, pastoring a local church and resting safe at home in bed with her every night. But she knows that God has a purpose for everything, and she has come to understand that Don's ministry revolves around NASCAR, doing what he can to touch lives with the grace and love of Christ.

"Besides," Cyndee says with a barely perceptible smile, "I realize now that the life I knew as a little girl was preparing me for the life I was going to know as a wife and mother. What seems to others on the outside to be so hard seems natural and normal to me because that's the way my childhood was."

117

Don believes that God was showing his great wisdom in giving him Cyndee to be his life's partner. She is the perfect complement to Don's personality and hectic lifestyle.

Cyndee sees it this way: "I'm a calming effect on him. I can bring up his sensitivity. Though Don is naturally sensitive, in his rush and businesslike attitude, sometimes he can plow over people and things. So I like to work on bringing out his sensitivity."

Because Don moves so fast, she believes that he is prone to doing or saying things without thinking them through completely.

"Sometimes," she says with a laugh, "I'd like to have a little pause button that I could push to make him stop for a moment and think carefully before he said something." Occasionally, when she replays for Don something he said, explaining the way it hit her or might have struck someone else, he says, "Oh, no—that's not what I meant at all." And when he sees that he was wrong about something or has unintentionally hurt someone's feelings, he's quick to apologize. His willingness to say he's sorry is on her list of one hundred reasons, and she says it is one of her husband's most endearing qualities.

"Despite the fact that he sometimes moves a little bit too fast, I love his energy. He can come in a room and it brightens up just because he's there. That's what happens in our home after he's been gone for a few days."

She also believes that one of her most important roles in Don's life is serving as his "pastor," his spiritual partner.

"Don's job in NASCAR, though it doesn't pull him away from his faith, doesn't replenish that faith, either. The focus is not on living a Christian life at the track. So that's where I see my role, too, when he comes home—to help him get back to the basics, to refuel and refocus."

One of the few things Cyndee regrets about being married to a man who spends so much time in the spotlight is that it often puts her in the spotlight, too, and that's the last place she wants to be.

"If the kids and I go somewhere alone—to a restaurant, a store, or to church—we can go in and out unnoticed. When we

118

go with Don, we're not able to do that, and it's hard for me. I like to be more private. I prefer not to be noticed coming or going, so I don't like the attention Don receives when it spills over into his and our private lives in situations that have nothing to do with NASCAR."

It makes Cyndee feel good to know that Dale Earnhardt is sensitive to Don's family and that he would like to find ways for Don to stay home more often. "But really, what can he do? Not a whole lot. It's kind of like a doctor who's on call so often, and his hours are so long. You really can't do anything about it. As long as he has this position and he's involved in NASCAR, there's nothing anyone can do to change it.

"But knowing Dale's attitude helps because it reinforces my own feelings about worth to the family."

And so, if she can't do anything about her husband's frequent absences, she uses them. Or more accurately, God uses them to build in her the fruit of the Spirit—especially patience.

"You know, life is not easy and fair or always fun, but I have learned to rely more heavily on the Lord when Don isn't here and I'm dealing with a difficult situation. I have nowhere else to turn but the Lord."

And he is always there.

Randall on Hawk

Danielle Randall, Pinnacle Racing Cards: Don Hawk is a very hard-working, caring individual. I consider Don to be completely trustworthy and have found him to be just as interested in what we are doing to meet our objectives as he is in meeting his objectives.

The man must wear tennis shoes out like crazy because he's so busy. If I could, I'd give Don about four more assistants, for two reasons. First, so he could spend more time with his family, because I know how hard it is in this business to find time

119

for your family. Second, so the man could have a breather every once in a while.

The driving force behind him, I think, is his love for his family first and the sport of auto racing next. Don's also a Christian, and I know he's touched many people's lives in motor sports who maybe weren't necessarily open to certain ideals of Christianity. Don, by his actions, is able to plant seeds in people's minds that, maybe, wouldn't have been planted apart from his example. God works in mysterious ways, and I think that within NASCAR, he is working through the person of Don Hawk.

What I'd most like to say about Don is that he's been a joy for me to work with for the past several years, and I look forward to doing business with him in the future.

What It's like Working for The Intimidator

Darlington, South Carolina

Dale Jarrett's dream of a million-dollar payday has dissolved into the cold reality of crumpled sheet metal almost as quickly as a race fan can say "oil slick." A large patch of oil in the 47th lap of the Mountain Dew Southern 500 on this "track too tough to tame" has robbed him of the magical seven-figure payoff this Labor Day weekend.

A victory here would have made Jarrett only the second driver ever to win the big prize for his performance in the four races that make up the Winston Select Million. At first it looked like he was a cinch. He roared out to a lead which he maintained for most of the early going. His car was clearly the fastest on the track, and the crowd was already on its feet, cheering him on.

Rusty Wallace stayed close behind, giving it everything he had in an attempt to catch up to Jarrett as they flew into the difficult third turn at Darlington's egg-shaped oval. Several other cars were bunched in a pack a couple of car-lengths back.

None of the drivers saw the large oil slick in their path—including Jarrett. His Ford Thunderbird hit the oil at 150 miles per hour and careened into the wall. Wallace spun out of control, along with several other cars, which went slamming into each other and the wall. No one was seriously injured, but it took several minutes to untangle the wreckage and restart the action.

Jarrett continued, but he lost three laps while making nine pit stops. His crew performed heroically in an effort to keep him in the race, but there was just too much damage and too much for them to do. They replaced a broken shock, repaired a control arm, ball joint, and damaged panels on the right side of the car—all at record speed. But all that time in the pit took Jarrett out of contention. Although he did manage to finish the race, he had to settle for fourteenth place, two laps behind eventual winner Jeff Gordon.

Twenty-five-year-old Gordon was far enough behind the leaders that he could take evasive action when he saw the others hit the slick, and he went on to his third straight victory here by winning a tight battle with Hut Stricklin. Dale Earnhardt is the only other driver to win three in a row at Darlington in forty-seven years of racing here.

After the race, Jarrett said, "I wasn't pushing it. I was just running a comfortable pace when I hit the oil and went right into the wall.

"I guess someone must have dropped some oil and no one saw it until it was too late. I was out in front, right where I wanted to be because that's usually the safest place. But unfortunately, being out there got me the first guy into the oil."

Wallace said, "It all happened so fast no one had a chance."

Gordon, who won $99,630 and averaged 136 miles an hour in his multicolored Chevy, said, "The old-timers say you have to have luck at Darlington. I think we had it today. I'd been running up front with Jarrett when we made our first pit stop. It was a bad one, and when we got back out we'd fallen to sixth or seventh. If we'd come out second or third, we'd have been in that oil slick with the leaders. As it was, I was able to slow down a little and escape it."

Although Jarrett failed to win a million dollars, he did earn a consolation prize of one hundred thousand dollars for winning two of the four races—at Daytona and Charlotte.

Down but Not Yet Out

This year's race for the Winston Cup championship seems to be shaping into a battle between Jarrett, Gordon, and Labonte. With the season winding down, it's not going to be easy for Earnhardt to win the eighth Winston Cup title of his career.

Still, it's much too early to count him out. If there's one thing the other drivers on the circuit have learned, it's that Earnhardt is never defeated until it's over—and that's true of a race or an entire season. There's no such thing as a comfortable lead against Dale Earnhardt.

He's dangerous. The Intimidator. The Dominator. He perpetuates the image with his black Monte Carlo, his dark clothing, and his ever-present sunglasses.

Don Hawk is often asked what it's like to work for such an enigmatic character. His answer is that it's just great. And then he says, "I think the Earnhardt mystique is something that he has perfected over the course of years, and I think it helps his performance on a racetrack.

"I heard Darrell Waltrip say the other day that whoever first called Dale Earnhardt 'The Dominator' was making a terrible mistake. He didn't mean that it was incorrect to think of Earnhardt as 'The Dominator.' What he meant was that once Dale had that nickname, he believed it, started reeling off championships, and hasn't stopped since. Waltrip said, 'I'd like to shoot the guy who gave him that name, because Dale started believing it and driving like it.'"

Drivers constantly give each other nicknames, sometimes out of legitimate respect and honor, sometimes because they are picking at each other in jest. Rusty Wallace started calling Earnhardt "Ironhead" because of the tough, slam-bang way he drives. Earnhardt returned the favor, and Wallace now bears the nickname "Rubberhead" with good-natured pride.

During the 1995 season, when Jeff Gordon, then twenty-four years old, was on his way to the Winston Cup championship, Earnhardt nicknamed him "Boy Wonder." He also told reporters, "If the kid wins the championship, he's so young they won't be able to serve him alcohol" at the year-end banquet.

Gordon didn't forget that comment, and he was ready when the time came to receive the championship trophy during an elegant banquet at New York's Waldorf Astoria. As Gordon sat at the head table, the waiter approached with a quart of milk in an ice cream bucket. With great ceremony, he filled a champagne glass to the brim with the white liquid and handed it to Gordon. "Boy Wonder" stood up, raised his glass high, and announced to the crowd, "I'd like to toast Mr. Earnhardt, because he requested this toast." In response, Earnhardt stood up with his champagne glass raised high, and the entire room rang with loud laughter and cheers.

The Man in the Mirror

Some drivers won't admit what others acknowledge—that their attitude and their approach to the next lap change when they look in the rearview mirror and see the black Number 3 car gaining on them. That same mystique works off the track when some of Earnhardt's competitors, especially newcomers to NASCAR, are intimidated by the way Earnhardt dresses and carries himself.

Hawk says it's not an act. "It's the real Dale Earnhardt people see, not a fake. He doesn't dress the way he dresses to be somebody he's not. Dale used to wear boots and jeans before he became the famous race-car driver that he is. He didn't change his style of living as his popularity grew. Every day, it's pretty much the same thing—Wrangler jeans, Justin boots, and Wrangler shirts. I think he's pretty down-to-earth that way."

124

What Don admires most about Earnhardt is his integrity. "He's extremely honest. A lot of people don't pick that up. He's so honest that some people are bothered by it. They think he's being 'smart.' He's not. He's just being honest."

Honesty, of course, is one of the things Don has always demanded of himself and his employers. The integrity of Dale and Teresa Earnhardt is one of the primary reasons why he is so comfortable working for them.

Don is also amazed and impressed by Dale's attention to detail and his ability to be listening carefully when it seems that his mind is a thousand miles away. One afternoon in Earnhardt's office, when Dale was exhausted after another long racing weekend and was stretched out on the couch, Don was going over some business.

Don says he was going on and on about the small details of a proposed contract from a company that wanted Earnhardt to appear in a couple of commercials and make some public appearances. Earnhardt lay quietly with his hat over his eyes. It occurred to Don that his boss was asleep, so he quit talking and prepared to put the contract back into his briefcase.

After a moment of silence, Earnhardt asked, "Now, was that two commercials and three public appearances, or three commercials and two public appearances?"

Don got the papers back out and went over the details again, amazed that even in his exhausted state, Earnhardt had been listening after all.

"When you're at the racetrack and you want an interview with him or you want to talk to him, he may look like he's upset or angry. He might even look like he's not listening to you—but if he isn't, it's not because he's being mean or because he doesn't care. It's simply because his number one focus is the race that lies ahead and how he can win it. He's more concerned about that than ensuring that a reporter from some magazine or TV station gets the quote or the sound bite he's after.

"The hardest thing for a lot of people who deal with Earnhardt is knowing when it's the right time to talk with him. What I've had to do with Dale is just what I had to do with Alan Kulwicki. You have to learn to read their faces and their eyes, to understand their body language. Only then can you know if it is a good or bad time to talk with them. It doesn't matter to Dale, just as it didn't matter to Alan, if you're bringing a million-dollar deal their way. If the face says, 'Don't talk to me now,' it's best not to open your mouth. You just have to learn to read the signals."

Don says that he seldom discusses business with Dale at the track. "If something comes up that's extremely important, I'll tell Teresa. If she thinks it's important enough, she'll tell him right away. She can read him better than I can."

Talk to Him after the Race

Don can peg Earnhardt's responsiveness after a race to what happened on the track. "After the race, if he wins he'll give everybody as much as they want for as long as they want. If he finishes second, you'll get fewer sound bites and not as much time. Third place, you'll get a smile but not much in the way of talking. From fourth place on back, we're heading for the airplane right away. We're out of there."

The only time Earnhardt is happy to finish other than first is when he is driving a car that, by rights, should finish farther back but that he and his team improve enough to come home in, say, third instead of twelfth. It makes him feel good to know that he and his crew have worked so well together as a unit and that he has "driven his tail off to finish eight or nine spots ahead of where he should've finished with the car," Don says.

In 1991, Earnhardt was running fourteenth going into the final 10 laps of the Busch Clash. He passed four cars on the next lap—leaving nine cars to overtake in the 9 remaining laps. He needed only 2 laps to leave them behind, and he went on to win.

"No matter what size track he's on, if Dale is anywhere within striking distance with 10 laps remaining, he's gone," Don says. "That doesn't mean he'll always win, but he's going to get the fans on their feet and give them a show."

Hawk remembers with amazement a time in Bristol when Earnhardt wrecked and the crew had to cut off the front end of the car. "We had bungee cords holding things together and kneepads and gloves for support underneath the radiator. With that car, Dale held his ground."

Another time on the same track "he had an altercation with Rusty Wallace and hit Rusty's car. NASCAR penalized him . . . sent him to the back, so he drove through the whole field to the front again. His car was having trouble soon after that, and he faded all the way back to the rear, only to drive through the pack a second time."

Before he was done that day, Earnhardt found himself at the back of the field a third time, but "he muscled up to the front again, hit Terry Labonte crossing the finish line and just about won the race, finishing second."

Don says "I think Dale likes to do what the fans think is impossible, and he thrives on the challenge. It's another one of the keys to the Earnhardt mystique."

Aggressive, Not Malicious

Though Don admits his boss is aggressive, he adamantly maintains that there is nothing malicious about the way Earnhardt races or lives. Earnhardt was known as a scrapper early in his career. He'd do whatever it took to win, including banging and scraping his way to the finish line. His driving style made him an expensive proposition for any car owner because he wound up wrecking so many vehicles. It also made him the object of anger from his fellow drivers. But it won him many races and earned him a reputation as a force to be reckoned with on any track.

Earnhardt remembers in particular one early Friday-night duel for third place on a dirt track with Stick Elliott, Bill Elliott's father. Going into the last lap, Earnhardt recalls that he "got right up on old Stick's bumper and caught hold of him just right and spun him around just as pretty as you'll ever see." After the race, Earnhardt was getting out of his car when someone hurried up to tell him that one of Elliott's mechanics was coming after him with a pistol.

"I ran out of there, jumped over the wall, and ran off."

The next Friday night, Earnhardt was waiting for a drivers' meeting to start when he looked up and saw Elliott approaching him, accompanied by several crewmen.

Earnhardt thought he was in for a fight, and he was clearly outnumbered. But Elliott simply smiled, folded his arms across his chest, and said, "You know, you just might make a driver yet."[9]

Earnhardt drove the same way when he joined the NASCAR ranks, and it was a style that prompted Darrell Waltrip to say, "With Earnhardt, every lap is a controlled crash."

The jury may still be out on whether Earnhardt has mellowed over the years. He's still capable of slamming and banging his way to the checkered flag, but now that he's an old pro, his tactics aren't considered to be the arrogance of an upstart.

"Dale is not malicious," Don says. "I don't think he ever hits anybody on purpose. I really don't. I can't speak for what he did eight or nine years ago on a dirt track somewhere, but I can just tell you that on a high-speed racetrack racing for points, and knowing the danger of the sport, he doesn't hit anybody on purpose."

Don acknowledges that the nature of the man is so competitive he might bump a car and nudge it to move on and pass.

"Yes, I think that happens. He does not, however, say to himself, 'I'm going to come up on this guy, hit him, and knock the heck out of him and go on.' That is not Dale Earnhardt.

"Some of the best racing I've seen since I've been with Earnhardt has been when Rusty Wallace and Dale have been side by side, just beating and banging on each other. One of them finishes first, one of them finishes second. Or one finishes third and the other fourth, and when they get out of their cars at the end of it all, you'll never see two bigger smiles than the ones on the faces of those two guys.

"Watch for it the next time you see a televised race or you're at the track. The minute those two get side by side, the crowd just stands up because Rusty's not afraid to exchange sheet metal or get bumped going into a corner with Dale, because he trusts him.

128

"And Dale trusts Rusty. They both know that neither of them will do anything stupid out there. I think that's important. There are other drivers who share that same comfort level with Dale when they're racing against him, and for the same reason. They recognize the danger in the sport and they're smart enough not to do anything foolish on the track."

Still, even though Wallace may relish a challenge against Earnhardt, he has been known to bounce a water bottle off his opponent's head after a particularly tough confrontation. *Car and Driver* magazine says of Earnhardt: "[He] is a throwback to the reckless days of NASCAR racing in the 1950s. He projects aggression even in the way he sits in his black Chevrolet Monte Carlo.

"He slouches low in the car, sitting in a side-low-backed bucket seat that has none of the braces and wraparound supports of the latest safety-engineered seats. He prefers single-width seatbelts to double-width, and he wears an open-faced helmet. His cheeks, his nose, his mouth, his sandy-brown mustache—all are exposed to what may come.

"This flies in the face of the latest in racing safety technology. But Earnhardt is certain his way is safer. He can see better with that open-faced helmet, he says. Besides, his competitors can see his face.

"'They know whether I'm happy or glad or sad or mad,' he says. 'I like to look over at a guy and grin at him.'

"Enjoy him while you can, because it will be somebody else's world before his kind comes along again."[10]

Childress on Hawk

Richard Childress, owner of Mr. Goodwrench car #3, driven by Dale Earnhardt: I've known Don for quite a number of years, back to the time he first got into the sport with Alan Kulwicki, and I consider him a friend. He is someone who has a reputation for honesty and integrity in this sport, and he's carried those traits to new dimensions. He's always trying to look at the sport from the standpoint of helping to improve it in anything he does. Instead of just signing any contract that comes along, Don works quality deals, and anything he does, he does first class.

I think Don has been really good for Dale Earnhardt. He came along at a time when Dale's career was on the upswing and he needed a Don Hawk to help carry him to a new level in marketing and a lot of other areas.

One thing that I've noticed about Don as I've observed him over the years is that he not only always does the right thing, but he helps a lot of people because he's always so full of life and so upbeat. I've only seen him get down maybe once or twice in all the time I've known him, and he never stays down. He's the kind of guy who, no matter what the situation, will find the bright side. If we have a bad day at the racetrack, or something like that, he'll come over, slap you on the back, and say, "Next week. We'll get 'em next week!"

Getting Ready for Race Day

Richmond, Virginia

Ernie Irvan has taken a page from Dale Earnhardt's book to earn his second victory of the year—winning The Miller 400 at Richmond International Raceway. And in the process, Irvan has scrambled the point standings for the Winston Cup championship with slightly over a month to go.

Irvan stayed within striking distance for most of the race, and then put on a burst of speed with 19 laps to go, passing Johnny Benson on the first turn and blazing home to victory, while the capacity crowd roared its approval.

The triumph is another step in Irvan's remarkable comeback since his nearly fatal accident at Michigan International Speedway in 1994. During the last eleven races after his return to racing, Irvan has finished in the top five eight times. His streak includes a second-place finish in the prestigious Brickyard 400 at Indianapolis Motor Speedway.

"Boy Wonder" Jeff Gordon finished second today, falling just short in his bid to sweep the year's series of races at the three-quarter-mile oval.

Earnhardt and his team are left making another quick exit after the race. There is no time to worry about finishing out of the money here. Next Sunday brings another race and another chance to climb a notch in the Winston Cup standings.

First, You Qualify

"If you want to understand what makes Dale Earnhardt tick," Don Hawk says, "you've got to know that when he goes to a racetrack, he's got his mind set on one thing, and that's qualifying first. That's done on Friday, unless we go to a track where we qualify earlier in the week.

"He's not worried at that point about his race setup; he's just focused on his qualifying setup so he'll be able to go as fast as he can for one or two laps—whatever the event calls for—to qualify.

"He changes gears on Friday night. If we qualified poorly, he may want to requalify. But before he does that, he'll ask himself what can be gained by requalifying. Does he think the car can go faster than it did the first time? Or he may want to just stand on his time because he feels that during the race he can pass all the guys who've qualified in front of him. He has to make decisions about all of these things.

"If we qualify well enough on Friday that we don't have to worry about trying a second time on Saturday morning, Dale's attitude when we get to the track is, 'Give me a race setup. Let me run a bunch of laps. I want to see what this car does under race conditions.'"

On Saturday afternoon before a Sunday race, NASCAR drivers conduct what is called Happy Hour, a final one-hour practice session.

132

Don says, "My name for it is Show and Tell. When you go out there, you want to run the best you possibly can because you know everybody's watching. This is your chance to show how tough you're going to be on Sunday. When Dale goes out there, he'll typically do one of two things. Either he'll get in front of a line of cars right from the start and drive like a man possessed so no one can pass him, or he'll go to the end of the line, pass them all on his way to the front, and then shut off the car and tell the guys to take a plug check before he parks it for the night.

"To me, that's a part of his mystique. He's given them all something to think about and left them wondering, 'Is that how strong he is for sure? Is he holding anything back?'"

Often, Earnhardt will cut short his last practice session, put the car in jack stands, cover it, and make his team the first one out of the garage.

At home that night, his attitude changes again.

"Now it's totally intense and race, race, race," Don says. "If we've qualified well, he's thinking, 'How can I get to the front and lead as many laps as possible?' If it's a short track, it's 'How can I save my equipment as long as I can, still knowing that I have to grab five points and lead a lap somewhere along the way—and grab ten points if I can lead the most laps?'

"Dale is the best in the business, in my mind, at protecting and not using up a race car on a short track like Martinsville, Bristol, or Darlington.

"People see him move up from 26th position to 3rd and then just ride there, so they think, 'Oh, man, he's done. He's spent. He's got nothing left.'

"Well, he hasn't said this to me or anybody I know of, but after watching him all these years I know that between, say, lap 250 to 350, he gets himself into a rhythm, saving his brakes, saving his tires, saving his equipment.

"He'll let the leader get eight, ten car lengths away, but he'll always keep that car in sight, and Dale's a master of knowing how many pit stops he has left, and what he has to do to win the race.

"Then, with about seventy-five miles to go, the man's on a mission. All you have to do is take a stopwatch to Earnhardt and watch him go."

Hawk says Earnhardt has a phenomenal memory, which serves him well on the racetrack and in his business.

"If I tell him I have an order of something coming in on a certain date, he'll remember it, and I can be sure that when that date rolls around, he's going to ask me if the shipment came in.

"In the same way, when he comes in for a pit stop, he knows exactly what he needs. For example, the guys in the crew will be thinking that he needs two tires, and he'll know that he needs four.

"He'll get ready to pit and somebody will say, 'You've got seventy-six laps on this set of tires,' and he'll say, 'No, I've got seventy-four laps on this set because we ran two laps under caution and I pitted on the second one.' Then whoever he's talking to will say, 'Oh, yeah, Dale, that's right. You have seventy-four laps on that set of tires.' He has an unbelievable sense for that kind of stuff."

The Eyes of a Hawk

Another thing that makes Earnhardt such a formidable competitor is his amazing eyesight.

Don laughs when he remembers an event that happened at Martinsville, although it wasn't so laughable at the time and could have been tragic.

"It's a half-mile track that just constantly makes you dizzy because you're going round and round in circles and the track is so small.

"Well, in the middle of this race, Dale radios in to us in the pit crew, 'The tractor trailer is on fire. You'd better get somebody to go over there and put out the fire.'

"We all turn around, and sure enough, the compressor on the tractor trailer is on fire. Immediately, we see Teresa Earnhardt and Judy Childress [Richard's wife] come running out of the trailer. They were sitting in there watching the race on television while listening to the transmissions between Dale and the pit crew. That's when they learned, from the man who was driving around in circles as fast and furiously as he could go, that the trailer they're sitting in is on fire, and it might be a good idea if they got out."

At Dover Downs International Speedway, which is one of the toughest and most demanding of all NASCAR tracks—so tough it has been nicknamed the Monster Mile—Don remembers, "Dale is going through turn two when he looks off to his left, through the fence, through the garage area, into the back of our trailer and says to Richard Childress, 'Richard, what is your pilot Jim Cook doing eating again in the back of the truck? He's fat enough already.' About a minute after that, Cook comes running up to the pits and says, 'I don't believe he saw me standing there making a sandwich in the back of the trailer.'"

It's not easy, at 150 to 200 miles an hour, to be focused on anything other than the race at hand and, especially, the section of track immediately ahead. Somehow, Earnhardt manages. He will often get on the radio and instruct his crew, "Tell NASCAR there's debris in turn two, and it looks to me like it's a brake caliper."

Don says, "So we tell NASCAR, but they're not as quick to respond to such a message as you'd think. The reason is that some teams will report debris on the track when there isn't really any, just to get a caution flag and a needed pit stop.

"But if Dale reports something on the track during a race, and NASCAR doesn't believe him, he'll say, 'They might not want to throw a caution, but when somebody hits it and wrecks, tell 'em, I told 'em there was a brake caliper lying there.'"

Sure enough, the radio will come back on after the debris is removed. "Dale, NASCAR called in. Thanks a lot. They picked up that debris. You were right. It was a brake caliper."

Don says, "Other guys may be doing the same thing, but I don't know about it because I'm not with them. I do know what Dale does because I hear it, watch it, and admire it."

135

Mr. Fix-It

Don also admires Earnhardt's mechanical ability.

One evening Don was working on his son's go-kart in a garage at Earnhardt's farm. John had entered some go-kart races, and Don was trying to make the vehicle easier to handle.

"I was working on it, and, admittedly, I wasn't going too fast. I knew what I was doing, but it was probably going to take me four or five hours to get it done."

Earnhardt came in and watched for a while. After a few minutes, he said, "Let me help you with that."

The two of them worked together for a bit longer, but eventually, Earnhardt ended up doing the work while Don watched.

"He did the whole thing in forty-five minutes. He just started welding on it, moving things around, and everything he did made perfect sense. He thought of things that never would have occurred to me. It was pretty amazing.

"Dale is like that. It doesn't matter if it's a bulldozer, a tricycle, or anything else. He just has a knack for fixing things.

"I've seen him come into the garage when someone was working on one of their cars, and he'll take over and do it himself. He doesn't make you feel like you don't know what you're doing or anything like that. He just wants to help you.

"When he's working on something, he takes care of all the details, and that's true whether he's working on a mechanical problem or working with me to put together a business deal."

Don used to teach his auto mechanics an old motto: "You can only expect what you inspect."

He calls Earnhardt the epitome of that motto.

"He inspects everything, with the result that he doesn't miss much. Whether it's a five-dollar deal or one for a million dollars, it will be examined. The smaller deals get the same scrutiny as the larger ones. He makes sure the quality is there, or nothing is going to happen.

"Dale has a long-range picture in his head. He's not only thinking about today's business. He's thinking four, five, even ten years into the future. I don't know a lot of guys with as little education as Dale claims to have who think that far ahead and make decisions today that are going to affect them ten years from now.

"But Dale's not thinking so far ahead that he misses today. He capitalizes on every hour of the day. He's an early riser and works long hours."

Earnhardt often will take fifteen- or twenty-minute "power naps," and after that "he can go strong for another five or six hours," Don says.

Slow Down, You Move Too Fast

Don often is asked if Earnhardt's racetrack persona carries over into his driving on public streets and highways. In other words, does he drive like a maniac? The answer is absolutely not.

"Usually, when we go somewhere together, I'm the one driving," Don says. He admits to getting so engrossed in the conversations that he'll sometimes drive a bit too fast, drawing a caution flag from Earnhardt.

"He'll say to me, 'Don, slow down, you're going to get a ticket. Relax!'"

Don calls Earnhardt "an exceptionally good driver, whether he's on the track or behind the wheel of the family car. He's always thinking ahead, but when he drives, if he's going fast, he's never going dangerously fast because he's in control—always in control. If he's fishing, he's in control of the rod. Hunting—he's in control of the gun. Even in his planes, he tells the pilots where to go and how to get there. They're flying the Lear jet or the King Air, but if he wants to go someplace other than the destination on the flight manifest, he says so and they make it happen."

When word got out that Don was considering working for the Earnhardts, several of his friends warned him against it. They said Dale and Teresa were too tough and too demanding and suggested that his stay with them might not last long.

"I know now that they are demanding, but that's because they want you to do things right," Don says. "That's biblical, too. For

137

example, the parable of the profitable servant comes to mind . . . you know, the one who works his head off and he's wondering, 'Am I beating my head against the wall?' Well, sometimes you beat your head against the wall because you're paid to do what you're doing.

"They're not the type of people who are going to come in every day, pat you on the back, and say, 'Great job. That's the greatest deal I've ever seen. Way to go.' But the more I get to know them, the more I realize that they show me how much they appreciate me by the way they treat me and demonstrate trust and confidence in me. That means more than if they patted me on the back all the time.

"So it's a growth process for me and for them. As we get closer together, we're starting to understand each other more. I think Dale and Teresa know I don't work just for money, and I now understand they don't want someone who's just after a dollar.

"They want somebody who cares about them, who'll protect their name, interest, rights, and trademarks. That's the person they're going to put a lot of confidence in."

As Don sees it, he's in a unique situation. "Five years ago, I never would have guessed that I would one day be associated with a man like Dale Earnhardt or an organization like Dale Earnhardt Inc. I'm glad to be here and be part of the success.

"I believe that in the last three years, I've helped Dale and Teresa move to higher profit levels with their business interests. That's part of what I was hired to do, and everything has been done with integrity, honesty, and ethically, because neither Dale, Teresa, nor I would have it any other way."

Don says that for the first six or eight months after he began working for Dale Earnhardt Inc., Dale or Teresa always traveled with him on a business trip. They wanted to sit in on the meetings and watch how he handled the negotiations—how he countered proposals, modified submissions, or politely said no. These days, he travels alone.

"When I get on an airplane for a trip now, and go off to California, Arizona, Dallas, or anywhere else to negotiate a business deal, Dale and Teresa don't think that I'm going to commit them to something they won't like. They're comfortable, now, that I'm going to get them a contract that won't compromise their integrity or hurt them down the road.

"They still look at and review every piece of every deal I bring home because they're the ones in control, and that's how it should be."

Do I Really Want to Do This?

Arriving at that comfort level in his working relationship with Dale and Teresa wasn't always easy. Don admits there were days when he asked himself, Do I really want to do this?

Before linking up with the Earnhardts, he had the freedom and ability to make his own decisions. That he was not permitted such freedom in the Earnhardt organization but had to check everything with Dale and Teresa wore on him. He knew he was smart enough to make those calls, and he chafed under their "wait till we all get together to talk about it" attitude.

Three years after joining the organization, Don takes that "wait" response as a compliment, because the circle that once was so tightly closed around the Earnhardts now includes him. Few decisions are made without the three of them sitting in a room together.

Don's value to Dale Earnhardt Inc. is measured most by those times when he doesn't agree with the other two. He likes to quote Benjamin Franklin on this: "When two men are in business and they always agree, then one of them is unnecessary."

Because Don isn't a yes-man, he often votes against proposals and ideas that Dale or Teresa fully support. When he does, he explains to his boss, "If I always agree with you whenever you put something on the table, you don't need me. Go hire somebody else at half of what you pay me to move papers around for you."

Don says he loves what he does for the Earnhardt organization and he'll continue doing his job until it ceases to be fun. Only then will he find another job—teaching, perhaps, or a position in another sports organization, such as the National Basketball Association.

He says two things could drive him away from the Earnhardts, but he honestly doesn't think either of them will ever happen. The first would be if his integrity were questioned unnecessarily. The second would be if his bosses "suddenly stopped seeing the total picture"—no longer realizing that what the three of them have done together is just the beginning for Dale Earnhardt Inc.

Asked if there is anything about his boss that Don thinks the world ought to know, he nods.

"Dale is far more charitable than most people will ever know. And even though I'm not sure he'll agree with what I'm about to say, I think it's important that I say it. Dale and Teresa Earnhardt are biblically charitable. By that, I mean that Dale very often doesn't let his right hand know what his left hand is doing.

"He's helped people buy tires so they could get into a race. He's helped people pay their bills and expenses at the track, knowing that they didn't have a sponsor. And he almost always does things like that anonymously. He'll tell me, 'Don't put my name on the card, and don't tell 'em it came from me.' And I never have, until now."

Punch on Hawk

Dr. Jerry Punch, CBS and ESPN television announcer: If I could change one thing about Don Hawk, I'd have him move a little closer to me so we could spend a little more time together with our families. He's the kind of person I like being around because of the way he lives his life—with the same kind of family values and atmosphere that I cultivate in my family. That's why we've become friends.

I keep waiting for someone out there to take advantage of his kindness and generosity. Fortunately for him and Dale, Don Hawk is such a good negotiator that even if he walks into a meeting as the lamb, he comes out the winner. Or to use another biblical analogy, no matter how many times Goliath walks into the room to do battle with Don, Don is always the one left standing!

The Long and Winding Road

North Wilkesboro, North Carolina

It looks like the Boy Wonder is going to make it two Winston Cup championships in a row.

On a windy autumn afternoon, Jeff Gordon has breezed to victory in the last race ever to be held at the North Wilkesboro Speedway. It is his third consecutive win and his tenth of the season. Gordon has won four of the last five races, and has finished no lower than second in any of his last seven races.

He came into North Wilkesboro holding an 81-point lead over Terry Labonte and increased the margin to 111 points with his victory. Four races remain as NASCAR's "long and winding road" nears the end of its season.

Gordon, who started on the outside of the front row today, stayed with the front-runners the entire distance as the lead changed hands seven times. He led on 207 of the 400 laps and was ahead of the pack for the final 79 laps.

141

Gordon told reporters later, "I'm really glad we won, not just because this is the last one at North Wilkesboro, but because it's so slick and hard to win on."

Labonte was philosophical about his fifth-place finish: "We missed it today. The car was just a little bit too loose all day long."

The Team That Prays Together . . .

After the race, there was a bit of good-natured banter between Dale and Don.

"Hey, Don," Dale teased, "I guess your prayers aren't as strong as they used to be."

"What are you talking about?"

"Well, you prayed with me before the race, didn't you?"

"Of course. I always pray with you before the race."

"Then how come I didn't win? I guess your prayer didn't work."

"Didn't work? You're still in one piece aren't you?"

Dale and Don pray together often, for a good race, for the safety of all the drivers involved, for God to be honored in their lives. They do not pray for a victory.

"One of the things about Don that I liked right away," recalls Dale, "was his Christian faith. I also appreciated that we had a common heritage, both of us being Lutherans."

Earnhardt admits that he and Teresa had been looking for someone of Don's caliber to head up their business operations for several years, so "I guess it's true that the Lord sent him to us."

"Don and I have prayed together many times in the past several years. And, really, since 1982 Teresa and I have grown closer to God and become more involved in the things of our church. We're not always able to attend church, since we spend just about every Sunday during racing season at the track.

"But because we feel strongly about our own faith, Don is a welcome addition to the team. He's helped us grow stronger in our own faith, and we always pray together before a race. Teresa usually joins us, and it's really a neat thing."

Earnhardt says one of the things that interested him about Don from the start was that he had been to Bible college and was open about his faith.

"In this business, it's really important to have someone working with you who is honest and fair. And because of his Christian attitude, Don is a great negotiator. He has a knack for bringing people together, helping them work out their differences. He's able to step back, look at problems, and make the best of them as he works them out."

A Family Man Who Can Drive

Earnhardt also appreciates Don's devotion to family. "Don knows that he'd be nothing without Cyndee. That wife of his is a special person. I know he's on the road with us a lot and I feel bad about taking him away from his family. Teresa and I talk about it all the time.

"I don't think there's anything more important to Don Hawk than his wife and kids."

Earnhardt admires the fact that Don is "a very energetic person, very outgoing when it comes to business. He wants to get in there, work out a deal, and make the best of any program or situation he has. He always looks at the positive side of a proposal—what it can bring to the company—but there's always that part of him that will question, 'Well, wait a minute. Is this really good for the big picture?'"

As much as he admires Don's business sense, Dale is quick to admit that it wasn't only Don's business acumen that landed him a job with Dale Earnhardt Inc.

"More than that—it was the way he drove," Dale recalls with a laugh. He still remembers the trip to the airport after the Pocono race the first weekend Dale, Teresa, and Don got together.

"When I saw the way he drove and the shortcuts he knew, well, I knew he was the man we'd been looking for.

"I said, 'Don, you've got to come to work for us. No doubt about it.'"

According to Earnhardt, Don looked surprised and asked, "What made you make up your mind so fast?"

"Simple. You can drive!"

Earnhardt smiles. "I wasn't kidding either. Not much, anyway. I mean, getting out of Pocono can be a real nightmare, and he got us out of there pretty fast. I think he could drive on the racetrack if he had a mind to."

Don did have one distinction Dale and Teresa weren't sure about at first, Earnhardt admits.

"Teresa and I used to talk a lot about Don being from the North and all—you know, a Yankee. He's a little more—he calls it 'rammy'—I guess you'd call it 'feisty' than we are. But it's something we've become accustomed to, and it's never been a problem when it comes to the three of us working together.

"We rely on Don so much now, and Teresa and I are both very comfortable with him. He's helped me hire and do almost everything in the company since he joined us, and he's been a big part of the whole picture.

"Everybody down the line who's joined the team since Don has been right on the mark, and Don put each one of them in place. He's been a real asset to this company."

So What Should We Call You?

Earnhardt didn't have a title in mind for Don when he hired him.

"He was our business manager at first, and then, as the company started to take shape, he became the president of Dale Earnhardt Inc. As president, he oversees all the aspects of the company, including Dale Earnhardt Chevrolet and Sports Image. He's third in command, and everybody understands that Don is as much the boss as we are.

"He's really an asset to me at the Chevrolet dealership, because he understands the bottom line.

"Tom Johnson is a very qualified part-owner of the dealership and general manager. He's been instrumental in building

144

the dealership into what it is today. But Don gives me someone in-house here who is able to read the financial statements and company printouts. That makes it better when Tom, Don, and I get together for a meeting, because we understand what's going on before Don and I even get there.

"I know that everything we have came out of our accomplishments on the track, so I can't spend a lot of my time worrying about business. I put racing first, after family, and it's got to be that way. I put racing before the dealership, before the souvenir business, before anything else. Don understands that, and I tell you, we turned out to be a pretty strong team. There's no telling how far we can all go together."

Asked to sum up his assessment of Hawk, Earnhardt is succinct and sincere. "He's a winner. He knows what he wants and he goes after it, just like I do in a race. Don gives 110 percent. He's number one in my book."

Smith on Hawk

David Smith, crew chief, Childress Racing Team: I think of Don as a Christian brother because I know the Lord Jesus Christ as my savior. Still, I'm impressed with his business acumen, forthrightness, and honesty. I've known him for three or four years through his association with Dale Earnhardt.

I believe Don submits himself to the Lord and the precepts of the Bible and its teachings. First and foremost, he lives for the Lord. As a result, because Christ is the center of his life, the Lord puts Don's path and his thoughts in the proper order.

Since Don has been handling the business end of Dale Earnhardt Inc., I know that Dale has seen good things happen for his whole company. I believe that's because Don and Dale are both winners in life.

Dale is a winner on the NASCAR tracks and is terribly focused on being number one. Don takes that attitude in the business world. He's out to win, but again, it's a win-win situation when he deals with people.

Don's attitude is you're going to help us, but we're going to be able to help you at the same time. I think that's the way business relationships are built.

Down to the Wire

Concord, North Carolina

Today is a very good day for Terry Labonte and a very bad one for Jeff Gordon. The result is that now only one point separates them in the Winston Cup standings with three races left in the season.

First, Labonte's good day.

He won the UAW-GM Quality 500 by taking the lead from Mark Martin on the 308th lap and steadily pulling away to finish the 334-lap event 3.84 seconds ahead of Martin.

It's only Labonte's second victory of the season and his first in nearly six months, but his consistently high finishes have pulled him into virtually a dead heat with Gordon in the point standings.

Labonte will take home $133,950, after averaging just over 143 miles an hour on the Charlotte Motor Speedway oval.

Now, Gordon's bad day.

Whatever could go wrong did go wrong.

He stayed with the leaders throughout most of the early going before making an unscheduled pit stop on lap 176. His crew raised the hood and began pouring water into his overheating radiator. Gordon had been in third place when he stopped, but by the time he made it back out on the track, he had given up three laps to Labonte and the other leaders.

On lap 227 he lost more ground as he brushed up against the fourth-turn wall. Eight laps later, he received a one-lap penalty for passing several cars while making a caution-period pit stop. He crossed the finish line in 31st place.

What? Me Tired?

It's been a long-year for Don and Dale, and in many ways it's also been frustrating.

Frustrating, because at this point in the season, it seems highly unlikely that Earnhardt will be able to pick up enough ground to win his eighth Winston Cup championship.

By most people's standards, it's been a good year, with a number of victories and top-five finishes. But anything less than a first-place finish or a championship is something of a disappointment to a man like Dale Earnhardt.

Don is tired. He has to be feeling the frustration. But he doesn't show it. He's the same ball of energy as always. Up. Happy. Doing everything he can to encourage those around him. Always on the verge of another big deal.

Larry Hedrick, who was Don's boss in the early days of his NASCAR career, watches with bemused respect and admiration. "Don's a great guy who lives his creed. I remember a saying I read somewhere, I believe it was in *Apples of Gold,* that went: 'I'd rather see a sermon than hear one any day. I'd rather someone walk with me than merely show the way.'

"And then it goes on to say, 'While I may misunderstand you and the high advice you give, there's no misunderstanding how you act and how you live.'

"That's Don Hawk to me. Watch how he lives, and you'll see that his actions match up completely with his words. He's not one of those people who talk out of one side of the mouth and then act out of a different side.

"He's been a great inspiration to me—someone I can look up to and emulate."

Hedrick admires the way Don touches people with the love of Christ.

"He doesn't necessarily preach to them, quote Scriptures and such. He doesn't have to do it that way. They can see Christ in him just because of the way he lives and acts."

Because NASCAR people must spend Sundays at the track from February to October, there is no way for the drivers and race teams to attend church. So Motor Racing Outreach conducts chapel services before every race. Hedrick is active in the services and says, "I've seen our Sunday church services come a long way in the last few years. Not coincidental to all that has been Don Hawk's presence in the garage area at the same time.

"I'm not diminishing the work that Max Helton and Motor Racing Outreach have done. I just believe that Don brings a great deal of his high-road lifestyle to the religious and business aspects of NASCAR.

"His way of life is very high-road, and this is a very family oriented sport. As far as I know, NASCAR motor racing is one of the largest nondrug-using sports out there, and that goes for the drivers and the whole garage area."

Hedrick, who met Don when he had just begun working for Martin Birrane and hired him after Birrane folded his race team in the middle of the season, says, "If I could, I'd change his job from Earnhardt to Hedrick Motor Sports."

Remembering how he came to hire Don, Hedrick says, "I went to look at some of the equipment Birrane was selling. I saw that Don had an astute business mind, and that Martin's best interests were uppermost in his mind. Though Martin was in Ireland at the time, his affairs could not possibly have been handled better than they were handled by Don Hawk."

When Hedrick needed someone to manage his race team, "Don was the first man who came to my mind for a lot of reasons. I felt his enthusiasm for the sport and for life would bring a lot of excitement to our team.

"Also, the fact that Don and I are like-minded in terms of our relationship with Christ was another factor. He was a person who could bring some ethics and morals to our sport, and to our team in general.

"I think God wanted Don down here in NASCAR-land, because he let everything work out. Don came in and did a great job."

As he watches Don hurry past again, Hedrick smiles.

"There are a lot of things that make Don tick. You know, he's a competitive person, and I think that's probably why he has such enthusiasm for this sport. Don wants to be the best at what he does and takes pride in that. But without question, it's Don's competitive level that drives him."

Sam Bass, owner of Sam Bass Illustration and Design, a firm that does a great deal of work with NASCAR, appreciates Don's combination of business acumen and people skills.

"Don's a thorough businessman, but he's got a heart, too. He's very trusting and helpful. He's also involved with MRO [Motor Racing Outreach], so it's not just business, business, business with him. He's well-rounded. Don's not only looking out for what's good for Dale Earnhardt, but also what's good for the other people involved, and the entire sport of NASCAR racing."

Bass has never seen anybody who enjoys racing as much as Dale Earnhardt does. "And what a great thing it is for him to have a person he trusts to oversee the daily business routine.

"You know, Dale Earnhardt is the hottest property in NASCAR and has been for virtually ten years. Don has done a fantastic job working with Dale, and together they've become even bigger. It's amazing the magnitude and effect that Dale Earnhardt has on this sport.

"People go to the racetrack because they want to see a good race. If he starts at the back of the field, it's incredible to watch him come up through people. If he starts at the front, it's something to watch him fend off the other drivers.

"Everybody out there knows that Dale's one of a kind; a unique talent, and Don's representation has made his appeal and his presence in the sport even more established and powerful. That's really saying something."

To Bass, the championship qualities of Earnhardt underscore Don's worth. "Dale Earnhardt knows what he wants and how to get it. For him to put the kind of faith he has in Don's abilities says incredible things about Don Hawk, because not everybody gets Dale Earnhardt's blessing.

"Don has it, and that's probably the biggest compliment he could be given."

Hillin on Hawk

Bobby Hillin Jr., driver of Jasper Engines car #77: I met Don when he was conducting chapel services at the auto races and working with the Wood brothers. I was impressed with his excitement, his enthusiasm, and we became friends. I talked to Don about what I was trying to accomplish in racing, and our friendship just grew.

I don't know if he does this with Dale, but the single biggest thing I appreciated about Don when I worked with him was that he had an ability to sense what a person needed at a particular time. I remember in particular something he always used to do before a race. He would find a meaningful quote and write it out on a piece of paper with a note about how it applied to what I was facing on that particular race day, or what we were trying to accomplish as a team. It was always something to help get me focused, to give me a better perspective on what we were doing, or to provide extra motivation.

Epilogue

Hampton, Georgia

The final race of the year, the NAPA 500 at Atlanta Motor Speedway, has turned out to be a day the Labonte family will never forget.

Bobby Labonte has won the race, earning his first victory of the season.

Older brother Terry has won the Winston Cup championship with a mere thirty-seven points over Jeff Gordon by placing fifth. It's his twenty-first top-five finish of the season.

Bobby led the first six laps of the race before being passed by his brother, who was in front of the pack for the next two laps. The brothers continued to trade the lead while Gordon lost two laps with a damaged left rear wheel.

By midrace, both Labontes had experienced problems of their own and fallen back into the pack.

Then both drivers began to charge.

On lap 286, Bobby passed Ricky Rudd to move into second. He maneuvered past Bobby Hamilton on the next lap to take the lead, which he maintained for the final 42 laps.

When Bobby took over the lead, Terry was in eighth place and began making some moves of his own. By lap 300 he made his way into fifth place. Knowing that was enough to give him the Winston Cup championship, he was content to stay there for the rest of the afternoon.

153

When the race was over, the jubilant brothers drove side-by-side in a victory lap.

Terry Labonte later declared that the race was "the longest of my life, but we did what we had to do."

A Good Year, but Not Good Enough

Dale Earnhardt ran a good race and crossed the finish line in fourth, which netted him fourth place in the yearly standings.

Still, the season was not ending on a good note.

Earnhardt was winless in the last twenty-seven races of the year, his longest streak without a first-place finish in twelve years. And anything less than a championship is not quite good enough for The Intimidator.

NASCAR experts were surprised that Earnhardt was able to have such a good year, especially considering the fractured collarbone and sternum he had suffered in the horrific crash at Talladega midway through the season.

For Earnhardt, though, there was one major consolation. He and Terry Labonte had been NASCAR rookies in 1979, when Earnhardt won Rookie of the Year honors.

"Congratulations to Terry Labonte. That's a good deal. I'm glad to see Texas Terry win—Class of '79!"

For Don Hawk, there is no time for a breather and no such thing as an off-season. There is much to do before the next season officially begins.

Don can't stop running—not even for a moment.

The Longest Road Trip

Two weeks after the Labonte family's dual triumph, a sea of flags bears the legend of Dale Earnhardt's number three. Thunderous noise rises from thousands of rabid fans who stand and try to cheer their favorite NASCAR driver to victory. People stand in line for hours to buy souvenirs related to their favorite driver or racing team.

Charlotte, North Carolina? Talladega, Alabama? Atlanta, Georgia? No.

Would you believe Suzuka, Japan? On a blustery November day, NASCAR racing takes another giant step forward by making an impressive debut in the Orient with the Suzuka Thunder Special 100.

The 140-mile race, which is separated into halves, turns out to be a duel between those two old slam-bang rivals, Rusty Wallace and Dale Earnhardt. Wallace, who lost the lead late in the first half of the race, regains it in the second half, passes Terry Labonte on the inside of the first corner, and winds up 1.2 seconds ahead of Earnhardt at the checkered flag. Wallace has won despite experiencing problems with his brake pedal throughout the race.

At the finish line, Wallace raised a hand high from his car window, displaying American and Japanese flags. Then, after parking his black Ford Thunderbird behind the winner's podium, Wallace climbed onto the car's roof and raised both fists high into the air, acknowledging the thunderous applause.

"It's a picture-perfect week for me," he said. "I won the pole and won the race."

All Dale and Don could do was adopt an attitude of "Wait until next year" regarding the Winston Cup season and the next race in Japan. If Japan's reaction to the Suzuka Thunder Special 100 is any indication, NASCAR could have a very big future here.

That means new possibilities and markets will open to Dale Earnhardt Inc.

For Don, it could also mean even more responsibilities, much more to do, longer trips, and extra time away from his family.

But that's part of the price Don will have to pay, because it also means new worlds to conquer—and more people to touch with the love of Christ.

That, more than anything else, is what Don Hawk is all about.

155

1996 Winston Cup Final Standings

Top Ten Drivers

Driver	Races Won	Total Points
1. Terry Labonte	2	4,657
2. Jeff Gordon	10	4,620
3. Dale Jarrett	4	4,568
4. Dale Earnhardt	2	4,327
5. Mark Martin	0	4,278
6. Ricky Rudd	1	3,845
7. Rusty Wallace	5	3,717
8. Sterling Marlin	2	3,682
9. Bobby Hamilton	1	3,639
10. Ernie Irvan	2	3,632

Notes

1. Ed Hinton, "Remembering Neil Bonnett," *Car and Driver,* May 1994, 40.
2. Ed Hinton, "Richard Childress: Good Guys Wear Black," *Sport,* July 1994, 195.
3. Shav Glick, "The NASCAR Boom," *Los Angeles Times,* April 30, 1996.
4. Suzanne Oliver, "A Fan-Friendly Sport," *Forbes,* July 3, 1995, 70.
5. Oliver, "A Fan-Friendly Sport," 72–73.
6. Glick, "The NASCAR Boom."
7. Ed Hinton, "Attitude for Sale," *Sports Illustrated,* February 6, 1995, 74.
8. Brett Honeycutt, "Stand and Deliver," *Sports Spectrum,* April 1997, 30.
9. Hinton, "Attitude for Sale," 72.
10. Bob Zeller, "The Best Finishes Second,"*Car and Driver,* March 1996, 124.

A Word from Don Hawk

A special word to my wife, Cyndee, my daughters, Jessica, Julie, and Jennifer, and my son, John:

Whatever success I have been able to achieve in NASCAR and with Dale Earnhardt has come at your expense. I know that. I was away from you far more often than I should have been. More than I wanted to be.

By allowing me to do my job, you deprived yourselves time after time of a husband and a father. Your willingness to share me at tremendous cost to yourselves in time spent together as a family demonstrates both your selflessness and unconditional love for me.

I want you to know that I am thankful for your special love. It is God's gift and your gift to me. I am humbled by it, and I want you to know how very much I love you.

A special word to Jerome Lucido:

I still find myself calling you Coach, because that is what you were to me when I first met you. You have always been a motivator, and I appreciated that. You express words and feelings with emotion, excitement, enthusiasm, and accuracy. But you have been much more than a coach or even a professor; you have been a great friend. Thanks.

A special word to Elmer Johnson, without whom this book would never have been published:

158

You discipled me even before my days at college; you encouraged me to go to college, and there you became a professor of mine. More than that, you became a great and trusted friend. You taught me how to invest some of my first savings; it was one of my first lessons in business. Through the years we have always talked; miles could not separate us. We talked golf, philosophy, marriage, babies, stocks, life, death, and mere Christianity. I even got you to start talking about racing.

You have played a big role in my life because you have been a true friend. You have loved me, rebuked me, encouraged me, and bragged about me. Thank you, Elmer, for your help with this book. But more than that, thank you for your help with my life. You believed in me.

Bickford on Hawk

John Bickford Sr., CEO *of Action Performance Companies and stepfather of Jeff Gordon:*

Perceived to be a ruthless negotiator.
In reality he truly finds the long-term value.
He is a man who looks you straight in the eye
  to talk about a problem or to say thank you.
He is a man who works relentlessly
  but stops to spend time with his family.
He is a man who gives of himself to others.
He is a true warrior.
He is my friend.

Jerome Lucido is a freelance writer of motion picture screenplays and magazine articles. He has taught English and journalism on the college level and has coached varsity athletics. It was while he was coaching soccer that he met Don Hawk. He and his wife, Bonnie, live in Allentown, Pennsylvania.